Federal Lending and Economic Stability

Federal Lending
and Economic Stability

By George F. Break

THE BROOKINGS INSTITUTION
Washington, D.C.

THE BROOKINGS INSTITUTION is an independent organization devoted to nonpartisan research, education, and publication in economics, government, foreign policy, and the social sciences generally. Its principal purposes are to aid in the development of sound public policies and to promote public understanding of issues of national importance.

The Institution was founded December 8, 1927, to merge the activities of the Institute for Government Research, founded in 1916, the Institute of Economics, founded in 1922, and the Robert Brookings Graduate School of Economics and Government, founded in 1924.

The general administration of the Institution is the responsibility of a self-perpetuating Board of Trustees. The Trustees are likewise charged with maintaining the independence of the staff and fostering the most favorable conditions for creative research and education. The immediate direction of the policies, program, and staff of the Institution is vested in the President, assisted by the division directors and an advisory council, chosen from the professional staff of the Institution.

In publishing a study, the Institution presents it as a competent treatment of a subject worthy of public consideration. The interpretations and conclusions in such publications are those of the author or authors and do not purport to represent the views of the other staff members, officers, or trustees of the Brookings Institution.

113705

Foreword

DIRECT FEDERAL LENDING has extended its influence greatly since the end of World War II. Only four major loan programs existed in 1946 but by 1964 more than a dozen were operating.

In the process of expansion, direct federal loan programs both helped and hindered efforts of policy-makers to keep the United States on a stable path of economic growth. The nature of these conflicting effects and their implications for future stabilization policy are examined in this study.

The volume reflects the Institution's continuing interest in financial institutions and credit policy represented by such earlier studies as *Money in a Theory of Finance,* by John G. Gurley and Edward S. Shaw, and *The National Debt Ceiling,* by Marshall A. Robinson.

The author, Professor George F. Break, of the University of California at Berkeley, wishes to acknowledge the generous assistance of Joseph A. Pechman, Director of Economic Studies, both in organizing the manuscript and in sharpening its focus. Many valuable comments and criticisms were offered by the reading committee, consisting of Lester V. Chandler, Sam B. Chase, Jr., Leo Grebler, Bert G. Hickman, and Marshall Kaplan. J. Martin Carovano collected and organized the statistical data with great skill and patience and carried out the necessary calculations. The manuscript was edited by Evelyn Breck with the assistance of Frances Shattuck. The charts were prepared by Fred Powell and the index by Adele Garrett.

The author is most grateful for all of this assistance but assumes full responsibility for the final product. The views expressed in the study are his and do not purport to represent the views of the staff members, officers, or trustees of the Brookings Institution.

Robert D. Calkins
President

January 1965
The Brookings Institution
1775 Massachusetts Avenue, N.W.
Washington, D.C.

Contents

Foreword   vii

1. Introduction   1

    Direct Loans and Postwar Debt Trends   3
    Direct Loans in the Federal Budget   4
    Direct Loans and Resource Reallocation   6
    Direct Loans and Economic Stabilization   7

2. The Economic Effects of Federal Lending   11

    The Monetary-Fiscal Effects   11
    The Primary Income-Output Effects   14
    The Fiscal Offsets   19
    Interactions with Monetary Policy   27
    The Incidence of Federal Lending   28
    The Welfare Aspects of Federal Lending   36
    Policy Questions and Issues   39

3. Global Trends and Cycles in Postwar Federal Lending   47

    The Postwar Period as a Whole, June 30, 1946-June 30, 1963   47
    Life Stages and Postwar Trends   51
    Postwar Cycles in Loans and Their Fiscal Offsets   55

4. Basic Behavioral Patterns   82

    Flexible Stabilizers   83
    Secondary Mortgage Market Operations with Treasury and
       with Private Funds   97
    Long-Lag Programs   111
    Federal Lending and Structural Unemployment   120
    Conclusions   125

APPENDIX A. Major Lending Program Summaries   128

Loans Restricted to Marginal Borrowers   130
Unrestricted Loans   143
Foreign and Defense Loans   155
Subsidiary Loan Programs   157

APPENDIX B. General Tables   159

Index   179

1

Introduction

DIRECT LOAN PROGRAMS are a controversial and somewhat enigmatic branch of the federal fiscal family in the United States. From total obscurity before World War I, they have risen to a position of prominence that has caused much comment, both favorable and unfavorable. Even their financial requirements are frequently hard to predict. In theory, a loan program is a self-financing enterprise that will often earn a profit. Yet some of the best-established federal undertakings of this sort still lean heavily on the public purse. To economy-minded legislators this can be a frustration of no small proportions. These financial obscurities, however, are simple indeed compared to some of the economic aspects of federal lending. While some experts, for example, rate the demand-creating powers of loans on a par with those of federal purchases of goods and services or federal transfer payments, others believe that lending has very little net impact on the economy. Still others feel that loans got into the fiscal family on false pretenses and should instead be placed in the equally important, but much more publicity-shy, monetary clan.

Whatever the appropriate classification for federal loans may be, their postwar growth from $4.2 billion outstanding in mid-1946 to $30.2 billion in mid-1963, and the important stimulus they have provided to such activities as residential building, exporting, and the construction of rural electric and telephone facilities clearly entitle them to serious consideration from many points of view.

This study, which concentrates on the potential contributions of direct loans to economic stability, is divided into three main sections. In Chapter 2, a theoretical analysis of federal lending provides both a framework for the next two sections and some answers to important policy questions, six of which are selected for detailed discussion at the end of the chapter. In Chapter 3, a broad, quantitative survey of

1

federal lending during the postwar period is combined with an inquiry into its impact on other federal activities, that is, on debt operations, other expenditure programs, and tax policies. These fiscal offsets, as they are termed, are a much neglected aspect of federal lending but one that must be considered in any realistic appraisal of loan policies. The desirability of loan sales during a period of underemployment, for example, depends very much on whether they do or do not permit federal expenditures that otherwise would not have been made.

Chapter 4 attempts to distill from the great variety of postwar lending activities those basic behavioral patterns that are most significant for the economic policy maker. Flexible stabilizers are distinguished from programs whose countercyclical powers are limited by long time lags; secondary mortgage market operations with private funds are contrasted with the pre-1954 program that was financed entirely by the Treasury; and the contributions, both actual and potential, of direct loans to the maintenance of a high-level, full-employment economy are assessed.[1]

While the study includes within its scope all direct federal loans, its focus is on the major, nondefense programs that are financed from general revenues. The one exception is the Federal National Mortgage Association's Secondary Market Operations Trust Fund, which has its own debt-issuing powers, but which is included because it is still subject to federal management and control. More independent loan programs, such as those under the Farm Credit Administration and the Federal Home Loan Bank Board, are excluded from consideration.[2] Altogether, some seventeen lending programs are analyzed in Chapter 4 and Appendix A:

Farmers Home Administration Loans
Rural Electric and Telephone Loans
Area Redevelopment Loans
National Defense Educational Loans
Export-Import Bank Loans
Federal National Mortgage Association Secondary Market Operations

[1] Supplementary statistical and analytical data are contained in Apps. A and B.
[2] For analyses of these see Ernest Bloch, "The Federal Home Loan Bank System," and D. Gale Johnson, "The Credit Programs Supervised by the Farm Credit Administration," in Commission on Money and Credit, *Federal Credit Agencies* (Prentice-Hall, 1963), pp. 160-318.

Federal National Mortgage Association Special Assistance Functions
Federal National Mortgage Association Management and Liquidation Functions
College Housing Loans
Housing Loans for the Elderly
Public Facility Loans
Public Works Planning Advances
Reconstruction Finance Corporation Business Loans
Small Business Loans
Small Business Investment and Development Company Loans
Disaster Loans
Veterans Direct Home Loans

All other direct loans are included in the basic tabulations of Chapter 3 but are not discussed separately, either because they did not play an important role during the postwar period or because, like foreign aid and defense production loans, their operations were dominated by national security considerations. A detailed list of postwar direct loan programs is given in Appendix B, Table B-1.

Direct Loans and Postwar Debt Trends

Between mid-1946 and mid-1963, when its indebtedness to the private sector was virtually constant, the federal government increased its direct loan portfolio by $26 billion—an average of $1.5 billion a year, adding up to a total increase of 620 percent of its initial holdings of $4.2 billion. As Table 1-1 shows, however, this rate of growth was exceeded by federally guaranteed private loans made for civil purposes, particularly those of the Federal Housing and Veterans Administrations. Moreover, it was only in the national defense category that direct federal lending outpaced its rivals. Direct civil loans rose by only 385 percent during the seventeen-year period, a growth rate that was almost identical with that of all private debt and well below all of the other growth rates shown in Table 1-1.

Whether such a growth rate is excessive is not at issue here. Rather, the study will be concerned with the contribution that direct civil lending, given its current and prospective levels of activity, can make to the optimum allocation of resources and to economic stability. The problems involved, which are described briefly in the remainder of

TABLE 1-1. *Amounts of Debt Outstanding by Major Type,*
June 30, 1946 and June 30, 1963

(Billions of dollars)

Type of Debt	June 30, 1946	June 30, 1963	*Percentage Increase*
Direct Federal Loans	$ 4.2	$ 30.2	*620*
Civil	3.4	16.5	*385*
National Defense	0.9	13.7	*1,420*
Federally Guaranteed Loans	6.6	79.8	*1,110*
Federal Housing and Veterans			
Administrations	5.8	72.5	*1,150*
Other Civil	0.7	6.6	*845*
National Defense	0.1	0.7	*600*
Federal Indebtedness to the Private Sector	217.0	216.1	—
Nonfederal Debt	160.6	802.3	*400*
Private	147.0	720.2	*390*
State and Local Governments	13.6	82.1	*500*

Sources: For direct federal loans, App. B; for federally guaranteed loans, George F. Break, *The Economic Impact of Federal Loan Insurance* (National Planning Association, 1961), and Treasury Department, *Federal Credit Programs of the United States Government, June 30, 1963* (mimeo.); for federal indebtedness to the private sector, *Treasury Bulletin* (November 1963), p. 70; for nonfederal debt, *Economic Report of the President*, transmitted to the Congress January 1964, p. 270.

this chapter, range in complexity from some relatively straightforward reforms in the budgetary treatment of federal loans to the delicate task of coordinating the lending, borrowing, and general monetary policies of the federal government.

Direct Loans in the Federal Budget

If one were to compare the 1962 budget expenditures of the two leading loan agencies in the Department of Agriculture, one might conclude that the Rural Electrification Administration (REA) was more active than the Farmers Home Administration (FHA) because its expenditures were $303 million, compared to only $240 million for FHA.

The true situation, however, was the reverse. In 1962 FHA disbursed $587 million, collected $373 million, and hence had a net outflow of loan funds of $214 million. REA, on the other hand, disbursed only $293 million, collected $136 million, and had a net loan outflow of only $157 million. All of this information is available in the Budget,[3] but the expenditure totals distort the correct relationship because REA is reported on a gross basis, with loan disbursements and administrative expenses making up its expenditure total, whereas FHA is partially reported on a net basis, with loan repayments and interest income subtracted from disbursements and administrative expenses in order to derive a net expenditure figure.[4] This source of confusion is gradually being eliminated from the Budget as more and more lending programs are shifted from the general fund (accounted for on a gross basis) to public enterprise funds (accounted for on a net basis). In addition to comparable expenditure totals, this change provides more, and better arranged, quantitative information about lending operations.

Direct lending programs have sufficiently distinctive economic effects to justify a separate and prominent place for them in the federal budget. Much progress has already been made in this respect, and what is needed now is mainly a more effective arrangement of the wealth of information contained in the budget document and its appendix. In Chapter 2, the establishment of a Federal Lending Account is recommended, an abbreviated version of which for fiscal 1962 would look as follows:

Federal Lending Account, Fiscal 1962
(Billions of dollars)

Expenditures		Receipts	
Loan Disbursements	$5.7	Loan Repayments and Sales	$3.1
Net Financial Investment (+) or Disinvestment(−)		+2.6	
Administrative Expenses	0.1[a]	Interest Income	1.0
Lending Program Profit (+) or Loss (−)		+0.9	

[a] Estimated for all programs on the basis of the relationship between expenses and net income for those agencies reporting separate expenses for their lending operations.

With their net expenditures of $1.7 billion, federal lending programs accounted for a substantial portion of the total 1962 cash deficit of $5.8

[3] In Special Analysis E on "Federal Credit Programs" in *The Budget of the United States Government, Fiscal Year Ending June 30, 1964*, pp. 365-75.

[4] The loan repayments and interest income of the Rural Electrification Administration are included in Treasury miscellaneous receipts and are not shown separately in that account.

billion. At the same time, however, they added $2.6 billion to the federal government's holdings of financial assets,[5] and hence their operations should be viewed in a different light from those of spending programs that make no, or very little, contribution to the government's net wealth. A major purpose of a separate lending account, to be included with the other Summary Tables in Part 2 of the budget document, would be to highlight these distinctive features.[6]

Direct Loans and Resource Reallocation

Whenever resources are shifted from one use to another by federal lending, it is important to know whether there is a net gain or a net loss to society. As a protection against the latter, it has frequently been suggested that the interest rates on federal loans should be made equal to the federal borrowing rate plus an allowance for administrative costs and losses on bad loans. The discussion in Chapter 2 indicates, however, that the federal borrowing rate is not a component of the relevant welfare tests and that to use it for that purpose would result in the overexpansion of loan programs with few social benefits and the underexpansion of programs with many. Therefore, the present practice of including Treasury interest costs in lending agency expenses should be discontinued, and program evaluations and reforms should be based on computations derived from private profit and lending rates that have been selected according to the type of federal loan being made. The specific nature of these computations is discussed in Chapter 2.

[5] In principle, the amount of bad loans written off during 1962 should be subtracted from this figure, but so far losses of the direct loan programs have been very small, less than $6 million a year on the average. See U. S. House Banking and Currency Committee, *A Study of Federal Credit Programs*, Vol. 1 (Government Printing Office, 1964), pp. 102-08.

[6] *The Budget of the United States Government, Fiscal Year Ending June 30, 1965*, Table 6, p. 46, makes a useful distinction between investment and operating expenditures, but its expenditure total for the direct lending programs is partly on a net, and partly on a gross, basis.

Direct Loans and Economic Stabilization

As economic stabilizers, federal loan programs have three distinctive characteristics:

1. A program with fixed terms of credit tends to have a built-in pro-cyclical reaction mechanism created by the impact of monetary policy on private credit markets. During boom times, when money markets are typically tightened, borrowers find government loans increasingly attractive, and during recessions, easy money conditions permit them to satisfy more of their wants from nonfederal sources. Whether this kind of cyclical sensitivity is desirable depends on the nature of the federal loan program. If its sole purpose is to fill a private credit gap that becomes significantly greater under tight monetary conditions, or if it finances activities of the highest social priority, procyclical fluctuations in its operations may well be justified. In all other cases, however, lending terms should be varied so that federal lending reinforces, or at least does not seriously offset, the countercyclical impact of general monetary policy.

2. While the granting of loans has expansionary economic effects that are similar to those of other types of government expenditure, loan programs also have the unique feature of a return flow of principal repayments. Unlike other program managers, therefore, lending officials have two ways in which they can adapt their operations to changing economic conditions. Not only can they expand or slow down the authorization of new loans, but they can also make use of loan contracts that permit the countercyclical variation of principal repayments. It is true that such contracts are still relatively unfamiliar, but the federal government has had some experience with their use. They will be discussed later in this section.

3. The existence of an important set of federal loan programs adds some leverage that the executive branch of the government can use in stabilizing activities, especially as a defense against recession and underemployment. Conservative congressmen, who often balk over increased transfer expenditures or reduced tax rates, may be more sympathetic to higher federal lending because it is a type of government investment and promises higher income in the future. These features

alone do not make lending superior to the other kinds of expansionary fiscal policy, but if it is not greatly inferior on economic grounds, its greater political salability may make it the most practicable alternative. Loan programs also give the legislative and executive branches together (or the executive branch alone if credit laws grant it sufficient administrative discretion) important monetary powers which may, on occasion, serve as a backstop to overcautious Federal Reserve policy. This does not mean that the government always knows best, but central bankers have been known to overemphasize the dangers of inflation and to underestimate the costs of underemployment; and when they do, a government that has its own lending operations can affect private borrowers in much the same way as would liberalized Federal Reserve policies.

To this list of distinctive features, which together do not place federal loan programs in an inferior position for stabilization purposes, many people would add the important qualification that, on the average, loans have a lower expansionary power per dollar spent than do other types of federal expenditures. This proposition is examined at length in Chapter 2, and the conclusion is reached that there is no a priori presumption in its favor. The question is an empirical one, and until the relevant evidence has been made available, there is no reason to regard loans as either inferior or superior to taxes or transfers as stimulators of private economic activity.

For the immediate future a more important question concerns the impediments that policy makers are likely to face in any attempt to vary federal lending countercyclically. Analysis of the postwar record in Chapter 4 identifies the following as the main sources of trouble:

1. Some programs have such long processing lags that they can contribute to economic stability only by building up backlogs of approved loan applications during prosperity and then releasing them early in recessions.

2. The economic effects of some of the most important loan programs are spread over a long period of time, and little can be done to adapt them quickly to changing economic conditions.

3. The beneficiaries of a government spending program tend to resist its cutback during periods of threatening inflation, and federal lending officials typically believe that their agencies should be im-

mune from the effects of tight monetary and fiscal policies.[7] In some cases, particularly in the foreign and defense area, such beliefs are fully justified, but in many other cases they are not. There are difficulties here, but none that are unsurmountable or peculiar to lending operations per se.

4. Some lending programs have to operate with credit terms that are either fixed by legislation or based on a formula that generates changes at excessively infrequent intervals.

Of these problems, only the second is relatively impervious to solution, and most long-lag programs do have some short-lag projects that can be accelerated or restrained for stabilization purposes. The potentialities for countercyclical action are there, and the loan programs to which it can successfully be applied are important enough to add materially to federal fiscal powers.[8]

As for the means of implementing these powers, some, such as variations in the terms on which new loans are granted, are sufficiently familiar to need no discussion here, but others, such as the flexible scheduling of principal repayments, are relatively untried. Loan programs could, for example, acquire some built-in flexibility by making repayments a function of the borrower's income, so that, on the average, they would be accelerated during good times and postponed during bad. Alternatively, loan contracts could be written so as to give the borrower the right to request repayment relief during a developing recession and to give the government the right to seek accelerated repayments whenever both the borrower's profit position and the general state of the economy justify such action. It may be noted in this

[7] A 1963 questionnaire sent to federal credit agencies by the House Banking and Currency Committee contained the following question: "Do the program objectives or nature of the economic activity warrant insulation against fluctuations in the private credit system or should the program be sensitive to general monetary and credit policy? "Almost uniformly the answers favored partial or complete insulation, the only exception among the major agencies being the Special Assistance Functions Fund of the Federal National Mortgage Association, which operates under a congressional directive to expand its purchases "as a means of retarding or stopping a decline in mortgage lending and homebuilding activities which threatens materially the stability of a high-level national economy." See *A Study of Federal Credit Programs*, Vol. 2, especially pp. 24, 45, 126, 299, 368, 556, 570, 643, 657, 795, 824, 832, 841, and 864.

[8] See the final section of Chap. 4 for a quantitative assessment of what could be accomplished by operating only with the most flexible of the federal loan programs.

regard that the Banks for Cooperatives relate repayments on their term loans to the gross sales of their borrowers.[9]

The sale of loans from lending agency portfolios may also be used to tighten private credit markets during inflationary periods, though extensive exploitation of these countercyclical powers would require legislation permitting sales at below-par prices. So far, however, federal loan sales have been concentrated in periods of easy money and excess unemployment. Given current budgetary accounting procedures and public attitudes toward federal deficits, procyclical sales of this kind are far from irrational, but, as will be shown in Chapter 2, they represent no more than a fourth-best solution to the problems at hand.

Policy makers throughout the government are finding federal loan programs both a challenge and an opportunity. They have a wide variety of tools available to them, but the forces they are dealing with are extremely complex and there are many gaps in the empirical evidence they need for guidance. Recent research has added considerably to their fund of knowledge about the operation of the various programs. The present study, by concentrating on typical problems and behavioral patterns rather than on the performance of individual loan programs, may, it is hoped, provide a different dimension to that knowledge. The reactions of borrowers and private lenders, as well as of the federal government itself to its own lending activities, are here analyzed in an effort to shed further light on the immensely complicated picture. Unless the direct loan programs are clearly understood, the fiscal planning of the future will not only become increasingly imprecise but it will be more and more subject to the hazard of thwarting its own good intentions.

[9] *A Study of Federal Credit Programs*, Vol. 2, p. 432.

2

The Economic Effects of Federal Lending

PUBLIC LOANS to private borrowers have several distinctive economic features. Unlike most kinds of government expenditures, loans are not directly income-generating, although indirectly, depending on the reactions of the borrowers, they may create as much income and output in the economy as an equal-sized public works project. Unlike government loan insurance, direct loans have an immediate budgetary impact, reducing the federal surplus or increasing the deficit unless offset by other fiscal actions. Unlike grants and gifts, government loans require the recipient to repay the original amount received, together with an interest rate that may range from a purely nominal one to one closely competitive with the rates set by private lenders. Public loans also differ from private loans by being restricted to carefully defined groups of borrowers, by granting relatively lenient terms (such as interest rates, minimum down payments, and maximum maturities) to the recipient, and by reacting in more complex and less predictable ways to changes in monetary policy. In the first six sections of this chapter, these distinguishing characteristics will be analyzed, and in the last section the results will be applied to six important policy questions.

The Monetary-Fiscal Effects

Disbursement of a government loan involves a transfer of money from the public to the private sector of the economy. The fiscal effect of this transaction, in the case of the federal government, is to reduce the Treasury's cash balance and, under present accounting procedures, to reduce the surplus or increase the deficit shown by both the administrative and the cash budgets. The monetary effects of the transaction is to increase the supply of money in private hands and, under a frac-

11

tional reserve banking system, to increase the lending powers of commercial banks. These money flows are of interest, not for their own sake, but because they set in motion a whole series of reactions, on the part of the loan recipients, the Congress, the Federal Reserve System and others, that alter the economic variables that are of concern in this study.[1]

The monetary-fiscal effects form, as it were, the economic foundation of the lending program, for without them the whole complicated edifice of price, output, income, and employment effects discussed below would collapse completely. Moreover, reliable measures of the monetary-fiscal effects of most federal loan programs are readily available, frequently on a quarterly basis, whereas quantification of the more important economic effects is a good deal more difficult. The policy maker, therefore, will be much concerned with the various kinds of money flows set in motion by government lending.

For purposes of this study, these flows may be classified into four main groups.

1. *Loan Operations on Capital Account.* Disbursement of loan proceeds (D) and the subsequent repayment (R) by the borrower of the loan principal are both balance-sheet transactions. To the government, disbursement means a reduction in its cash balance matched by an equal increase in its portfolio of private securities; and to the borrower, disbursement means an equal increase in his assets and in his liabilities. Principal repayments simply reverse these changes. In any given period of time, then, $D-R$ represents the net flow of government loan funds to private borrowers.

2. *Loan Operations on Income Account.* Like private lenders the government receives income (Y) from its borrowers in the form of in-

---

[1] Since bank reserves are effectively controlled by the Federal Reserve and the Treasury keeps most of its cash in commercial banks, the (potential) multiple expansionary effects of federal loans on private credit will not be considered further. The assumption, in other words, is that federal lending is not allowed to have any impact on commercial bank reserves that would not have been brought about by other means.

The economic effects "set in motion" by federal loan flows do not mean only those reactions that occur *after* the loan is disbursed. Many important effects will occur earlier, being induced by the anticipations created when a government loan is authorized, and these are included as well.

terest payments, fees, and service charges and provides income to others by hiring personnel, buying supplies, and in general making administrative expenditures (A). If no bad loans were ever made, $Y-A$ would measure the government's net income (or loss) from its lending programs.

3. *Portfolio Operations*. In addition to granting new loans, the government may purchase (P) loans previously made by private lenders, thereby shifting the securities in question from one portfolio to another. Conversely, the government may sell (S) old loans from its own portfolio to private financial institutions. Like the first category, these are balance-sheet transactions, this time entirely confined to the financial sector of the economy. Loan sales, of course, may result in realized gains or losses for the government's income account.

4. *Default and Liquidation Operations*. Default on a government loan affects lending operations on both capital and income accounts and introduces a final set of money flows between the public and the private sectors of the economy. In the first place, default stops the receipt by the government of both interest income (Y) and principal repayments (R) and provides instead whatever assets were pledged by the borrower as security for the loan. If the market value (X) of these assets is less than the outstanding principal of the defaulted loan (W), which will then be written off the government books, the deficiency $(X-W)$ becomes a loss to be deducted in the income account, together with whatever administrative expenses (A') are occasioned by the foreclosure and liquidation procedures.

Additional money flows will result from the sale by the government of the seized assets (X). Frequently, this will involve both the receipt of cash (C) and the granting of a new loan (D'), which in turn will result in a new series of interest receipts (Y') and principal repayments (R'). The total money flow to the government from its default and liquidation operations, therefore, is $C + R' + Y' - A'$, where $C + R' = C + D' = X$.

In summary, then, government lending programs give rise to a net flow of money from the public to the private sector which, during any given period of time, may be measured by:

(1) $TE = (D - R) + (A - Y) + (P - S) + (A' - Y') - (C + R')$, where

TE designates Treasury net money expenditures. Alternatively, if all loans are combined, including those made in the liquidation of seized collateral:

(2) $TE = (D + D' - R - R') + (A + A' - Y - Y') + (P - S) - X,$[2]

or more simply:

(3) $TE = (D - R) + (A - Y) + (P - S) - X$, where it is understood that the items in the first two sets of parentheses cover all types of loans made.

The Primary Income-Output Effects

The various kinds of money flows that result from government lending affect the behavior both of private individuals and of the government itself. The effects on the government, and the effects of these effects on the private sector of the economy, are taken up in the next section. Here the direct, or first-round, economic impact of government loans is considered—for example, the extent to which private incomes and output are increased by the granting of new loans but reduced by the repayment of old loans.

The simplest case with which to start is a loan extended to a borrower who either has been unable to obtain private credit or has been unwilling to do so on prevailing credit terms. In this instance, the entire amount of the government disbursement is an addition to the supply of funds in the hands of private spending units. Expenditure of the loan proceeds on newly produced goods and services, for example, will raise output directly, whereas expenditure of the proceeds on land and other existing assets will do so only indirectly, partly because the owners of existing assets will enjoy capital gains, and partly because higher prices on used assets tend to stimulate investment in new ones. Important as these indirect stimuli may be, they are, given the present state of empirical knowledge, much less predictable than the direct expansionary effects of loans used to buy new output.

The output-generating powers of government loans become more difficult to determine when those loans are granted to borrowers who

---

[2] Since D' is a noncash expenditure its inclusion in the first term must be balanced by its subtraction in the last, X being equal to $C + D'$.

otherwise could, and would, have obtained private loans, although presumably on more stringent terms and therefore in smaller amounts. Consider, for example, the disbursement of 100 to government borrowers who otherwise would have obtained 40 from private lenders. The government loans, therefore, add only an extra 60 to the funds of these borrowers, but at the same time they add 40 to the funds of lenders for potential disbursement to nongovernment borrowers. While 60 percent of such public loans may be analyzed in the manner suggested in the opening two paragraphs, the remaining 40 percent must be treated differently. For it, the question must first be asked: To what extent will lenders use their additional funds for loans to private spending units and then try to determine the extent to which the recipient spending units will use the loan proceeds to purchase new output? There is no need to dwell on the difficulties involved in these procedures.[3]

Government loans may also be used to refinance existing private loans, and if they are, their economic effects will depend on what alternative sources of funds the borrower would otherwise have fallen back on. If he would have repaid his private loan by reducing his expenditures on new goods and services, the government loan should be classified as fully output-generating, though in a special, *defensive* sense. That is to say, instead of financing an increase in private spending, it simply prevents a decline that otherwise would have occurred. Alternatively, the government refinancing loan might prevent the sale of existing assets by the borrower, or if it kept him from defaulting on his private loan, it would, in effect, expand the lending powers of private financial institutions.[4]

It is clear, then, that although government loans are capable—considering now only their initial impact and not a full multiplier-accelerator sequence—of raising GNP by the full amount of the funds disbursed, actual performance may fall significantly short of this mark.

[3] See, for example, James R. Schlesinger, "Monetary Policy and Its Critics," *Journal of Political Economy*, Vol. 68 (December 1960), pp. 601-08, and the Commission on Money and Credit, *Money and Credit: Their Influence on Jobs, Prices, and Growth* (Prentice-Hall, Inc., 1961), pp. 46-62.

[4] This last effect would also be produced by a government loan that enabled the recipient to repay his private indebtedness faster than he otherwise would have done.

Funds added to the private sector, in other words, may escape the main GNP output-income flow either by being used to purchase old assets or by being hoarded by the recipient. Such leakages, however, may be offset, more or less, by two countervailing stimuli. In the first place, the government borrower may add some of his own funds to those of the government in order to carry out a project that otherwise would not have been undertaken. While such additions may represent only a shift from the purchase of other kinds of new output, they may, in the proper circumstances, result in an important activation of the money supply. Secondly, government loans may induce private lenders to make additional loans to the same borrowers. If the funds in question would not have been loaned to other spending units, there is another stimulus to GNP, over and above the effects of the government loan disbursements.

There can be little doubt that the various initial, or primary, income-output effects of government loan disbursements present a complicated picture. Nor is the outlook much different when other aspects of public lending are considered. Loan principal repayments, for example, presumably have some deflationary impact on the private sector, but this impact need not exactly offset the effects of an equal amount of loan disbursements. If it does not, $D - R$ cannot simply be computed for a given lending program during a given period of time and that net monetary flow used as an estimate of the primary stimulus of the program to the economy. In principle, one could write the expression $hD - kR$ for the net income-output effect in question, but in practice the determination of the two marginal spending propensities, h and k, would be very difficult.

It is worth noting, however, that in some important cases k will be zero. Suppose that a set of government loans finances the construction of durable, real assets with resources that otherwise would have been either unemployed or devoted to private consumption, and that in later years, while the loans are outstanding, the real assets always provide government borrowers with enough gross income to cover whatever principal repayments are made to the government. In these later years, then, society has real assets that would not have existed save for the government loans; and the principal repayments, being so-to-speak self-financed, will exert no deflationary effect on the economy.

It is also true, of course, that instead of creating real assets, government loans may simply transfer ownership of a given stock from one group in the private sector to another. Principal repayments on such loans do have potential deflationary effects. Because of the repayments, funds are transferred from private spending units, that probably would otherwise have spent them on goods and services, to the federal government, which need not spend them. Nevertheless, a dollar left in private hands may simply sit there idly, and as will be shown below, the receipt of principal repayments may have some expansionary impact on government spending. One is well advised, therefore, to take a cautious and skeptical view of the deflationary powers of government loan repayments, and similar arguments apply to interest payments on government loans.

Purchases and sales of existing loans by federal lending agencies have effects similar to Federal Reserve open market operations and hence need no detailed discussion here. By these transactions private lenders are provided with more or fewer funds, and the impact on private production will depend both on how quickly and vigorously lenders react to their changed financial condition and on how sensitive private spending units are to easier or tighter credit terms. Lending agency administrative expenditures, in contrast, are fully output- and income-generating, apart from the occasional purchase of used equipment.[5]

It would be pleasant to be able to close this section by reporting that most, or all, of the economic effects discussed could be measured with reasonable accuracy. Unfortunately, such is not the case. In the absence of that ideal situation, however, a few guidelines can be set down that will be followed in the economic analysis of the specific lending programs discussed in Chapter 4 and Appendix A.

1. Loans to borrowers able to obtain private credit should be separated from loans aimed at marginal or submarginal borrowers.

2. The latter kind of loan concentrates its impact directly on the government borrower. It should be useful in these cases to consider the proposed uses of the loan proceeds, distinguishing the purchase of new output from the acquisition of land and used assets, and giving

[5] Here current national income accounting procedures are followed, and it is assumed that government administrative expenditures create output of equal economic value.

separate treatment to defensive, or refinancing, loans. At the same time, it must be recognized that the proposed uses do not always turn out to be the actual uses.

3. Although some uses of loan funds are not fully output-generating, the loans themselves may serve to activate private money balances. The existence of these offsetting possibilities immediately suggests the construction of minimum and maximum estimates of the primary economic impact of government loan disbursements. For the minimum, one could take only those loans obtained for the purchase of new output, and for the maximum, one could add to total government loan disbursements estimates of the amounts provided for the same projects both by the borrowers themselves and by other private lenders. Where such min-max boundaries are not feasible, one is at least entitled to the consolation that straightforward use of government loan disbursements does provide a middle-of-the-road estimate that will sometimes err in the one direction and sometimes in the other.

4. As already shown, both new government loans to borrowers with ample access to private credit and government purchases of existing private loans exert their economic influence through private financial markets. These transactions, then, should be combined and analyzed separately, with particular attention paid to the sensitivity of private demands to monetary changes during the periods of time under consideration.

5. While the excess of disbursements over repayments during a given period of time may be used as a first approximation to the net economic impact of a particular loan program, the two opposing money flows should be separated, at least for all major programs, since the expansionary effects of disbursements need not be exactly offset by the contractionary effects of an equal amount of principal repayments.

6. It should be stressed that only the primary income-output effects of government lending have been of concern here. A complete picture would have to include second- and further-round spending effects of the familiar multiplier and accelerator variety. Since these effects are not likely to differ for government loans from what they would be for other types of government expenditures, they will not be considered further.

The Fiscal Offsets

Like a government enterprise selling services to the public, a lending program may have no impact on government finances, or it may be either a net supplier or a net demander of funds. The no-impact case occurs whenever administrative expenditures and disbursements on new loans are exactly matched by interest receipts and principal repayments from existing loans. Apart from this special situation, however, government lending is likely to lead to fiscal actions which in turn will influence private spending behavior. Since both these actions and their induced income-output effects always oppose the fiscal and income-output effects already discussed, they will be referred to as the fiscal offsets of government lending.

The Range of Possibilities

Like any other kind of federal expenditure, loan disbursements can be financed in four ways: by the creation of new money, by borrowing from private investors, by reducing federal expenditures for other purposes, or by increasing taxes. Of these possibilities, the first appears not to be highly regarded in this country, and it would, of course, require the cooperation of the Federal Reserve authorities. Either the Treasury would have to borrow directly from the central bank, or if it borrowed from private investors, the Federal Reserve would have to increase the privately held money supply by the amount of the Treasury's bond sales. If this monetary expansion took the form of open-market purchases, there would, in effect, be no increase in the amount of federal debt held by the private sector, though there might be some change in its maturity structure. Such debt operations, however, are not an essential part of expenditure financing by money creation, the distinguishing characteristic of which is the absence of all fiscal offsets. A loan program financed in this way would, in other words, exert its full expansionary powers.

The other three methods of financing all reduce private incomes and output to some extent, except in very special circumstances. Higher taxes or lower government transfer expenditures reduce private spending by first lowering disposable incomes, the amount of the reduction in spending ordinarily being somewhat less than the reduction in incomes.[6] A cut in government purchases of goods and services, on the other hand, results in an equal cut in the economy's output, except where the funds would have been spent for imports or existing assets. It is the third alternative—the sale of government debt to private investors without the help of monetary expansion on the part of the central bank—that sets in motion the most complex deflationary effects.

In general, such debt sales tighten private money markets—raising interest rates, making such credit terms as minimum down payments and maximum maturities more stringent, and perhaps increasing the nonprice rationing of loan funds. As a result, the willingness and ability of private borrowers to consume and to invest are impaired. Nor are these the only deflationary effects. As interest rates rise, holders of bonds and other financial assets suffer capital losses and on this account can be expected to keep their spending propensities under closer check than they otherwise would. While private spending is restricted in these ways by both short-term and long-term debt sales, the latter are likely to have the greater effect, since they compete directly with the types of private securities used to finance such credit-sensitive activities as home-building and the construction of producers' durable plant and equipment.

To predict the effects of federal debt sales on Gross National Product, therefore, reliable measures are needed both of the sensitivity of lending terms to an increase in the supply of financial assets and of the responsiveness of private spending units to changes in credit terms and to capital gains and losses on financial assets. Empirical information of this kind has become increasingly available in recent years,[7]

[6] Recent official estimates place the impact on consumer spending between 92 and 94 percent of the change in disposable income. See the *Economic Report of the President*, transmitted to the Congress January 1963 (Government Printing Office, 1963), p. xvi.

[7] See, for example, Ralph Turvey's quantitative estimates of the impact of open market purchases and sales on federal bond yields in his *Interest Rates and Asset Prices* (London: George Allen and Unwin, 1960), pp. 60-78; Allan H. Meltzer's two articles on the determinants of the demand for money in the *Journal of Political Economy*, Vol. 71 (June 1963), pp. 219-46 and the *Quarterly Journal of Economics*,

but important gaps still remain. As a result, professional opinion ranges all the way from the view that debt sales have only minor effects on output to the view that they are capable of offsetting much of the expansionary thrust of fiscal policy.[8] My position is that debt operations do matter, and that debt-financed federal expenditures (or debt-financed tax reductions) can have significantly smaller expansionary effects than their absolute size would suggest.

The scope of fiscal offsets available to the federal government is clearly a wide one. At one extreme, by resorting to money creation, it may impose no offset at all and allow the loan program to exert its maximum expansionary pressure on the economy. At the other extreme, by cutting back its purchases of new output to make an equal amount of new loans, it may well more than offset the expansionary effects of those loans and end up with a net deflationary impact. Conversely, the net receipts from a declining loan program may be impounded in order to allow that loan program to have its greatest deflationary effect, or they may be devoted to such expansionary uses as the financing of net transfers to low income groups or the undertaking of new resource-using projects.

Federal Use of Fiscal Offsets

Recognition of this wide range of fiscal offsets immediately emphasizes the importance of discovering which ones the federal government has used in the past and which ones it is likely to employ in the future. Unfortunately, the wide dispersal of power within the federal government makes answering this question especially difficult. While the congressional committee authorizing the program, for example, may intend it to be financed by the sale of new Treasury debt, other parts of Congress may be so influenced either by the granting of the

Vol. 77 (August 1963), pp. 405-22; and such recent estimates of the interest-sensitivity of specific kinds of private spending as Frank de Leeuw's "The Demand for Capital Goods by Manufacturers: a Study of Quarterly Time Series," *Econometrica*, Vol. 30 (July 1962), pp. 407-23, and Tong Hun Lee's "The Stock Demand Elasticities of Non-Farm Housing," *Review of Economics and Statistics*, Vol. 46 (February 1964), pp. 82-89.

[8] For an excellent, nontechnical analysis of the powers of monetary and debt policies see John M. Culbertson, *Full Employment or Stagnation* (McGraw-Hill, 1964).

new loans or by the economic effects that follow that they cut back other federal expenditures or postpone the reduction of certain taxes so that in the end the loans are financed by these means rather than by debt issue. Nor does all of the control rest with Congress. The executive branch may finance one loan program by selling off the old loans of another, or it may react to the expansion of lending activities by slowing down the allocation of funds to some other expenditure program.

The only fiscal offset that can be established unequivocally occurs when a loan program is set up as a special (trust) fund with power to issue its own securities to the public but without access to Treasury funds. In all other cases, it is a matter of determining what Congress and the administration would have done had a new loan program not been inaugurated or had an established program not expanded or contracted when it did. A precise answer is obviously impossible. Nevertheless, one can identify certain sets of circumstances under which the use of one method of federal financing is significantly more probable than the use of some other method. The general nature of these circumstances will be indicated in the remainder of this section, and in the next chapter, the results will be related to the postwar period in this country.

The basis for this analysis is simple. First, suppose that in practice the size of the various federal tax and expenditure programs is based on the behavior of a limited set of economic and fiscal indicators. These need not be completely identified for our purposes, but they presumably would include such items as the rate of unemployment, the direction and amount of price level change, the rate of economic growth, and the size of the budgetary surplus or deficit.[9] For each indicator it is assumed that there is an acceptable range of values, indicating satisfactory fiscal or economic performance, and one or more unacceptable ranges whose occurrence would point to the desirability of taking corrective governmental action. For example, an unemployment rate of 4 percent or less might be regarded as satisfactory, whereas a higher rate would call for the adoption of expansionary fiscal policies. Moreover, it is recognized that the satisfactory-unsatisfactory ranges for the

[9] It should be stressed that the attempt here is to describe actual, rather than optimal, behavior. Many economists would feel, as I do, that the state of budgetary balance should not be a determinant of federal fiscal and monetary policy.

different indicators are likely to be interrelated. An unemployment rate between 4 percent and 5 percent, for instance, might be acceptable if the general price level is rising, but not otherwise. Other possibilities will readily occur to the reader.

Given that federal tax and expenditure programs are determined in this way, government loans will affect that determination by changing the relevant indicators. Provided these changes, taken together, are important enough, the fiscal impact of the loans should be concentrated on expenditures or taxes rather than on public debt operations. To see how this would work out in practice, consider a few of the basic economic situations likely to be encountered.

Suppose, to begin with, that the economy is in recession, and assume that, apart from the automatic stabilizers, recessions are combated at first by the expansion of federal expenditures, and only later, at some more severe stage, by a reduction in taxes. In these circumstances, more government loans will tend to moderate, or postpone, the countercyclical actions in question. For the most part, they do this by making economic conditions less unfavorable than they otherwise would be, but they may also do it by making the budget deficit larger—i.e. more unfavorable. The second effect is less certain because it is the result of two opposing influences which may reverse their relative importance as time passes. When they are made, of course, loan disbursements increase the deficit by the full amount of the money involved; but by making private incomes and output higher than they otherwise would be, the disbursements also reduce the size of the deficit, through the operation of the automatic stabilizers. Which of these two effects will dominate in any given period of time is a difficult question to answer, but ordinarily a steady flow of government loans may be thought of as giving rise to the following three-stage sequence of events:

1. In the first stage, the loans have already begun to expand private incomes and output, but no loan disbursements have yet been made. The budgetary impact of the loans, therefore, is to decrease the size of the federal deficit by some fraction, f, of the induced increase in private incomes.[10]

---

[10] Wilfred Lewis Jr. has estimated that during four postwar recoveries the built-in stabilizers reduced the deficit by 26 percent to 34 percent of the increase in GNP. See his *Federal Fiscal Policy in the Postwar Recessions* (Brookings Institution, 1962), p. 30.

2. In the second stage, disbursements are taking place, and the expansionary effects on income and output are building up according to the familiar consumption-investment relationships. If D is used to represent the flow of disbursements and hD is the increase in private incomes induced by the loans in this second period ($h \gtreqless 1$), the net impact of the loans on the federal deficit may be written as follows:

$$D - fhD$$

Since $f < 1$, $fhD < D$ unless h is sufficiently > 1. At this stage of the development of most loan programs, it may safely be assumed that h is not much greater than unity and hence that $fh < 1$. The conclusion then follows that the loans increase the size of the deficit in the second stage.

3. Throughout that stage, disbursements continue at a constant rate, but the expansionary effects on private incomes and output continue to increase—i.e., the size of h rises steadily. Therefore, the deficit-increasing effects of the loans become less and less, and eventually, if h increases sufficiently, the loan program will act to reduce the deficit.[11] At this point the third and final stage is reached.

Of these three alternating sets of effects, only the second can be counted on to last for a significant period of time. For many types of loans, the first stage will exist for only a few weeks, and quite conceivably consumption-investment relationships in the economy might be such that the third stage will never occur. The distinguishing feature of the second stage is that government loans affect both the economic and the budgetary indicators in the same way—namely, to reduce the attractiveness of discretionary changes in expenditure and tax programs. During the second stage, therefore, the chances are that the loans are *not* debt-financed. During the other two stages, these chances are weakened, though not necessarily significantly, by the fact that the economic and budgetary indicators are moved in opposite directions.[12]

[11] For a discussion of these possibilities, based on a multiplier-accelerator model, see Roy E. Moor's study for the U. S. Joint Economic Committee and published in their *1963 Joint Economic Report* (Government Printing Office, 1963), 45-55.

[12] Analyzed in the same way, the opposite case of an inflationary boom yields similar results. In this economic situation, more government loans accentuate the inflation and, during stage two, reduce the size of the budget surplus (or increase the deficit).

Suppose, next, that all of the economic indicators are firmly within their acceptable ranges and that the budget surplus, or deficit, is regarded as unduly large. A growing loan program would, in the one case, reduce the surplus and hence weaken the case for tax reductions or increases in other spending programs, and in the other, it would increase the deficit, thereby intensifying the need for corrective fiscal action.[13] To be sure, intensification of the need might give rise only to more, and perhaps louder, talk, so that in fact the Treasury would have to find the funds to finance the new loans by selling more of its own securities. As a counterbalance to this outcome, however, is the possibility that the loan program might trigger a tax increase, or expenditure reduction, considerably larger than the amount of the loans themselves.

Finally, consider a loan program that expands during a period when a major change is being made in the size of the public sector, involving parallel, but not necessarily matching, movements in both taxes and expenditures. A shift has occurred, in other words, in the society's desires for government services, and in our model, the accompanying change in taxes will not simply equal the change in expenditures but will be related to the expected behavior of the economic indicators. In this case, the loan program is very likely to end up by being tax-financed. If the major change is a reduction in certain spending programs, an expanding loan program will lessen the need for tax cuts to counteract the deflationary effects of the major change. Conversely, if the major change involves an expansion of government spending, the loan program will increase the need for fiscal offsets of a deflationary nature.

These examples indicate that federal loan programs financed from the general fund may well result in higher taxes or lower nonloan expenditures, rather than in greater sales of Treasury securities to private investors. Admittedly, to the accountant or the administrator, debt sales are probably the most obvious source of funds for a government loan program. For one thing, the government, in making loans,

---

As a result, both the economic and the budgetary indicators are moved so as to increase the need for tighter expenditure controls and/or higher taxes.

[13] It is assumed here that the loan program does not move any of the economic indicators out of their acceptable ranges.

acquires new assets, and this may be thought to justify the incurrence of new debt at least equal to the value of the new assets. Moreover, if the maturities of the Treasury securities issued are matched against the maturities of the federal loans made, repayment of the latter will come exactly when funds are needed to retire the former. Appealing as debt-financing may be on these scores, the standard procedure of financing federal loan programs from the general fund[14] cannot be viewed as guaranteeing the use of debt-financing. Indeed, if one had to select the most probable offset to federal lending during the postwar period, the choice would go, as will be shown in Chapter 3, not to debt sales but to a lower level of expenditures on other federal programs. The analysis there also shows, however, the great difficulties involved in making such choices, to say nothing of attempting to estimate the quantitative importance of the different offsets.

This discussion, therefore, ends on a negative note. Fiscal offsets to federal lending certainly exist, but they cannot be identified precisely in retrospect, and their use in the future cannot be forecast with confidence. Clear recognition of this situation, however, permits the drawing of two important, positive conclusions. The first is that, since individual fiscal offsets cannot be specified, the economic analysis of federal lending should begin by excluding all of them—that is, it should be based on the assumption that the loans in question are financed by money creation. Having thus determined what effects would emerge if there were no fiscal offsets, one can add the effects of whatever offsets, if any, are thought to be appropriate for the purpose at hand. In this way, separable actions are kept separate, the full potentialities of each are revealed,[15] and policy makers are presented with the entire range of possibilities open to them.

Secondly, since debt sales cannot be regarded as the typical source

[14] Typically in the form of loans made by the Secretary of the Treasury to the lending agency.

[15] Otherwise, it is all too easy to underestimate the effects of any one fiscal policy. From the past record, federal loans may appear to have only limited expansionary powers, whereas in fact their effects were always blunted in varying degrees by the operation of different fiscal offsets. To isolate the impact of federal lending, it is necessary not only to segregate the effects of concurrent changes in other federal expenditures and in taxes (as is frequently done), but also to eliminate the influence of Treasury debt operations during the same period of time (as is not commonly done).

of funds for federal loan programs, revisions are called for in the standard computations of program money costs. To lending agency administrative expenses (including expected losses on bad loans) is frequently added the interest payable on Treasury securities with maturities comparable to the agency's own loans,[16] but this last step is completely irrelevant whenever the loans are expenditure- or tax-financed. Nor, as will be evident later, is the Treasury borrowing rate likely to be a good indicator of a lending program's alternative opportunity cost.

Interactions with Monetary Policy

From its loan programs, the federal government derives monetary powers of no small magnitude, and one of its most important management problems is to integrate these successfully with the more general monetary powers of the Federal Reserve. A loan program with ample funds but with fixed lending terms, for example, would automatically offset the effects of Federal Reserve actions, since the demand for government loans in this case would increase when monetary policy was tightened and decrease when it was eased. Such a result is perverse from the point of view of general stabilization policy, but it could be defended by demonstrating that the particular sector of the economy served by the government loans is affected unduly severely by general monetary policy. In the absence of justification of this sort, such built-in procyclical variations in federal lending should be prevented by giving loan agencies both the authority and the obligation to vary their credit terms in line with changes in private credit markets, as recommended by the recent Cabinet Committee on Federal Credit Programs.[17] Nor would the administration need to limit itself to such passive cooperation with Federal Reserve policy. If it was felt, for example, that the central bank was unduly slow to react to a developing recession,[18] or unnecessarily cautious in its expansionary actions, fed-

---

[16] Such a procedure was recommended by the Committee on Federal Credit Programs, *Report to the President on Federal Credit Progams* (Government Printing Office, 1963), p. 26.

[17] *Ibid.*, pp. 8 and 39.

[18] Whereas the recognition lag, according to Fels, has averaged only four months

eral credit terms could be liberalized while private terms were remaining stable, or even tightening. By means of such policies, the supply of loan funds would be increased, and the countercyclical easing of private money markets accelerated.[19]

The Incidence of Federal Lending

Attention so far has been centered on the various ways in which federal loan programs can change the level of private demand for new output. The discussion will turn now to the allocative effects of those programs at some given level of national income, seeking to identify the different groups of people who are benefited or burdened by the change in the composition of output.[20] For this purpose, it is assumed that the primary income-output effects of the loan program are quantitatively, though not qualitatively, offset by the adoption of appropriately restrictive monetary or fiscal policies. If new loans of 100 are expected, for example, to bring about a first-round increase of 90 in the demand for new output, then quantitative balance can be achieved by simultaneous increases in taxes, reductions in other types of federal expenditures, larger sales of government debt to private investors, or some combination of these and other devices designed to reduce demand for new output by exactly 90. In other words, the discussion will concentrate on loan programs that are so managed as to have neither an expansionary nor a contractionary impact on aggregate demand—i.e.,

---

for postwar recessions, the lag in the switch of the Federal Reserve to easy money policy (since the Accord), according to Kareken and Solow, has averaged eight months. See Rendigs Fels, "The Recognition-Lag and Semi-Automatic Stabilizers," *Review of Economics and Statistics,* Vol. 45 (August 1963), p. 281; and John Kareken and Robert M. Solow, "Lags in Monetary Policy," in Commission on Money and Credit, *Stabilization Policies* (Prentice-Hall, 1963), pp. 67-73.

[19] A dynamic stabilization policy of this sort was recommended for the most flexible and expansionary types of federal lending by the Committee on Federal Credit Programs, *op. cit.,* p. 39.

[20] The concept of incidence is used by different people to mean different things. J. A. Stockfisch, for example, distinguishes five important effects of taxes that may be included under the heading of incidence: the income, price reallocation, spenders' welfare, incentive, and distributive effects. See "On the Obsolescence of Incidence," *Public Finance,* Vol. 14, No. 2 (1959), pp. 125-50. Here only the first three of these effects will be considered.

in the manner most appropriate under conditions of full employment and stable price levels. In this way, it is hoped that the allocative effects of government lending on individual prices and incomes can be brought into sharp focus.

It should be stressed at the outset that the kind of quantitative balance considered in this section is economic, rather than financial. Suppose, to continue the example of new loans of 100 with expansionary powers of 90, that a reduction in private demands of 90 can be brought about either by increased taxes of 95 or by increased sales of public debt of 110. In the first case, the government will have a financial deficit of 5 that must be financed so as not to reduce private spending, and in the second it has excess money receipts of 10 that must be handled so as not to increase private spending. What is required is that the deficit be financed by money creation and that the excess receipts be kept by the government and not returned to the private sector by the retirement of an equal amount of public debt. Balancing a given amount of loan disbursements with an equal amount of tax increases, expenditure cuts, or public debt sales does not, in other words, guarantee economic balance, and whenever the two diverge, it is assumed that economic balance will be given priority and that financial balance will then be achieved by the appropriate amount of money creation or destruction.

The major effect of an economically balanced loan program is to shift resources from somewhere in the economy into the hands of government borrowers, who are thereby enabled to enjoy whatever benefits can be obtained from the use of those resources. In the typical case, the government loan will finance part of a given project, and the borrower will contribute some funds of his own and perhaps also some of his own labor services. His gain from the loan may then be measured by subtracting from his income from the project both his interest payments to the government and the income he could have earned by putting his funds and labor services to their best alternative use. Conversely, those from whom the resources are shifted suffer losses partly because they have fewer resources to employ and partly because they may be forced to shift their own funds and labor services into inferior uses.

In addition to these primary benefits and burdens, any loan program can be expected to activate a complex set of price and income changes, some because the demand for certain products and productive services rises or falls, others because the price of a substitute or complementary item changes, and so forth. There is no need to discuss all of these effects in detail here.[21] Rather, discussion is restricted to the main features of the incidence patterns produced by the four available means of financing federal loans.

The Basic Pattern: Loans Financed by Money Creation

The incidence of an economically balanced loan program is necessarily a blend of the incidence of the loans themselves and that of the financial offsets used by the government. This blending is sometimes so perfect that the net result is quite different from its two component parts. In different circumstances, however, the two sets of effects intermingle very little and simply continue to exist side by side, each retaining most of its own distinctive features. This being the case, it is convenient to begin the discussion of incidence with the effects, at a given level of employment and real output, of government loans in isolation, that is, without the effects of any demand-reducing fiscal or monetary offsets. For this purpose, it is necessary to assume that the loans are made under conditions of full employment and are financed by the creation of new money. Since the burdens and benefits of such loans are an essential ingredient of each of the other incidence patterns, this first case will be referred to as the basic pattern.

For simplicity, the discussion will be confined to the consumption sector of the economy, and it will be assumed that the loans are used to purchase a particular type of consumer good, C_1, in the production of which only two kinds of factors are used, the first, F_1, being completely specialized to that industry and the second, F_{123}, having alternative employment opportunities in the production of consumer goods C_2 and C_3. Under the conditions assumed, both the price and output of C_1 will rise, and heightened competition for F_{123} will increase its price and draw some of it from industries C_2 and C_3 into the production of C_1. As this shift occurs, the prices of C_2 and C_3 will rise, and their output will fall.

---

[21] See, for example, Earl R. Rolph, *The Theory of Fiscal Economics* (University of California Press, 1954), especially Chaps. 6-12, and Arnold C. Harberger, "The Incidence of the Corporation Tax," *Journal of Political Economy*, Vol. 70 (June 1962), pp. 215-40.

Government borrowers, in short, attain their increased consumption of C_1 partly at the expense of other consumers of that product and partly at the expense of consumers of C_2 and C_3.

In addition to these immediate and direct effects, several others are worth mentioning. The reduction in the output of C_2 and C_3, for example, is likely to release from employment, factors usable in the production of other consumer goods, say C_4. As a result, more of C_4 can be provided by the economic system at lower prices, and owners of the shifted factors (F_{24} and F_{34}) will find their money incomes falling. Among owners of completely specialized factors, some, like F_1 and F_4, will gain, while others, like F_2 and F_3, will lose. In general, of course, money incomes are increased by the loan program, and an inflationary spiral may be inaugurated, to the detriment of such groups as net monetary creditors, pensioners, and others.[22] Finally, the whole set of buyer reactions to relative price changes may be noted—consumer demands increasing for products that are complementary to C_1 and C_4 or substitutable for C_2 and C_3 and falling for products of the opposite nature, and producers tending to substitute factors that have become cheaper for those that are more expensive.

How many of these effects would be different if the government financed its new loans by taxes with sufficient deflationary powers to offset the higher spending of government borrowers?

Coordinated and Uncoordinated Taxation

The most obvious accomplishment of higher taxes in the above context would be to keep the general price level stable and to prevent the development of an inflationary spiral. This could be done either by eliminating the upward price pressures of the basic pattern (coordinated taxation) or by allowing those pressures to develop but offsetting them by downward pressures on prices elsewhere in the economy (uncoordinated taxation). Let us relate each of these possibilities to the simplified example already developed.

Suppose, first, that the government levies an income tax whose only impact on private spending is to reduce the purchase of C_2. Demand for the transferable factor F_{123} is now subjected to opposing influences,

[22] For a summary of the redistributive effects of inflation see Martin Bronfenbrenner and F. D. Holzman, "Survey of Inflation Theory," *American Economic Review*, Vol. 53 (September 1963), pp. 646-52.

being higher because of the new government loans but lower because of the new taxes. It is conceivable, therefore, that F_{123} could be shifted from the production of C_2 to the production of C_1 without any increase in its own price and with no changes in the prices of C_1 or C_3. In any case, these prices will not rise as much as they would with new money financing, and as a result taxation of this type tends to concentrate the direct burden of the loan program on taxpayer-consumers of C_2 and to exempt from burden consumers of both C_1 and C_3.[23]

Suppose, next, that the new taxes reduce private spending only for C_5, a consumer good with no direct relationship, either in consumption or in production, with the loan-affected products C_1, C_2, and C_3. As producers of C_5 contract their activities, they reduce their demands, say, for some nonspecialized factor, F_{567}, pushing down its price and thereby providing an incentive for producers of C_6 and C_7 to expand output and to lower prices. These effects, of course, are simply the converse to those already described for C_1, C_2, and C_3 in the basic pattern.[24] While in one part of the economy government borrowers are gaining resources at the expense of consumers C_1, C_2, and C_3, in another part taxpayers are surrendering resources to the benefit of consumers of C_5, C_6, and C_7. It should be stressed that specific individuals can find themselves in more than one of these four groups.

Needless to say, few taxes, especially those levied on income, concentrate their spending impact on only a few products. It is readily seen, however, that a more practicable income tax would combine the features of the two hypothetical taxes just discussed. A restricted loan program that is financed by a general income tax, in other words, should raise the prices of products bought by government borrowers but lower most other prices,[25] whereas if both the loan program and the tax financing it are broad in scope, there should be relatively few price changes in either direction.

[23] Consumers of C_3, however, will bear some indirect burdens if the release of F_{24} from the production of C_2 induces an expansion in the output of C_4 and hence an increase in the demand for F_{34}.

[24] It should be stressed here that in order to consider the effects of a tax-financed loan program *at a given level of real national output*, it must be assumed that product and factor prices are sufficiently flexible downward to permit the maintenance of the pre-program level of employment.

[25] The income tax itself, of course, tends to make all prices lower than they would have been with the loan program alone.

Numerous other economic effects of tax-financed government lending could be discussed, but it is hoped that enough has been said to support the following general conclusions:

The primary economic burden of any loan program is restricted by the nature of the loans themselves to those groups using the same kinds of resources as the new government borrowers are demanding in the market place.

Within this group of potential burden bearers, which may be a large one, taxation can be used as an effective discriminating device, lightening the sacrifices of some while concentrating the burdens on others. Income taxation qualifies for this purpose as long as the loan program affects a wide range of economic activities, but when its impact is highly concentrated, selective excises should be more efficient.

If lending and taxing are not closely coordinated, the loans will allocate their burdens and benefits in one sector of the economy, much as they would have if they had been financed by money creation, while the taxes that finance them will impose their own burdens and benefits in some other sector. The principal accomplishment of taxation here is to stabilize both aggregate spending and the general price level. While the primary burden pattern of loans-plus-money-creation is not altered, the income redistribution that accompanies inflation is eliminated.

Debt-Financed Government Loans

Suppose next that the expansionary effects of government loans are to be fully offset by the sale of the appropriate amount of federal securities. What groups are likely to be affected in an important way by this method of financing?

Chief among the sufferers, of course, would be all other borrowers who, because of the debt operation, would be able to obtain fewer funds and on less favorable terms. The resulting reductions in spending, empirical evidence indicates, would mainly affect residential construction, state and local governmental construction, and business investment for purposes of modernization and increased efficiency.[26]

A second group made worse off would be holders of long-term

---

[26] Commission on Money and Credit, *Money and Credit: Their Influence on Jobs, Prices, and Growth* (Prentice-Hall, 1961), pp. 50-53.

bonds, the market value of which would fall as a result of the increased sales of federal securities. Some decline in private spending could be expected on this account, too, though its magnitude might not be great. Bondholders who were primarily concerned with interest income might not be fully aware of the capital losses they had suffered, and even if they were, the impact would be softened to the extent that they were in a position to take advantage of the higher rates of interest brought about by the federal debt sales. To do this, they would need only to have some liquid assets on hand or to be able to hold future consumption expenditures below the level of future income. Whether people would increase their rate of saving to an important degree is problematical. Higher-yielding financial assets are attractive, but they are not close substitutes for consumer durables or business plant and equipment. In normal circumstances, it is doubtful that interest rates would rise enough to induce widespread expenditure shifts of this sort.[27]

In general, then, a debt-financed federal loan program benefits one group of borrowers at the expense of another. If the demands of the two groups are similar, the shift of purchasing power between them should have little effect on prices; otherwise there will be both increases and decreases that will alter the real income positions of individual consumers and resource owners. Taken as a whole, private lenders should find their economic prospects improved, though they are subjected to opposing influences which may affect some of them differently from others. Federal loans, unless they are granted only to borrowers lacking access to private credit, reduce the demand for private loans; but federal debt sales have the opposite effect and, to offset the expansionary effects of the federal loans, would normally have to be carried far enough to create a net increase in the demand for private loan funds.

Interprogram Incidence

The final method of financing a loan program so as to achieve economic balance is by reducing government expenditures of other types

[27] For a detailed discussion of the deflationary effects of government debt sales see Earl R. Rolph, "The Incidence of Public Debt Operations," *National Tax Journal*, Vol. 9 (December 1956), pp. 339-53.

sufficiently to offset exactly the expansionary effects of the new loans. Burdens and benefits similar to those already discussed would result, their specific nature depending on the kind of federal expenditure that was eliminated:

If the expenditures in question financed government output of one kind or another, their reduction would release resources for potential employment elsewhere. As before, these resources may flow directly into the hands of government borrowers, or if they are not suitable for this purpose, they will go elsewhere, and government borrowers will be left to obtain their own resources by bidding for them against other potential users.

If government transfer payments are cut back in order to expand government loans, the effects will be essentially the same as if higher taxes had been imposed instead. In either case, private disposable incomes are reduced, and private spending should fall as a result.

New government loans may be made at the same time that old unmatured loans are sold off to private investors. This kind of portfolio switch has effects similar to those of debt-financing. Both operations involve the sale of financial assets on private markets, and lending terms there are tightened in the process.

The government may cut back one loan program in order to expand another. Here, there is simply a shift of funds from one group of borrowers to another, the impact on resource allocation depending on how different the spending plans of the two groups are.

Intraprogram Incidence

A few words should be said about the burdens of a self-financing loan program. Whenever principal repayments equal loan disbursements, old borrowers are in effect transferring funds to new borrowers. This does not mean, however, that old borrowers are bearing the burdens of the new loans. Regardless of whether they are better off or worse off as a result of their own government loans (and the former outcome is presumably much the more likely), old borrowers are not necessarily affected in any way by the government's decision to relend their principal repayments. To ascertain where the burden lies, the question must be asked: what would have been done with the principal repayments if the new loans had not been made? The answer, of course, is that taxes might have been reduced, other expenditure programs might have been expanded, federal securities might have been retired, or the money supply in private hands might have been allowed to fall. Since these fiscal actions are simply the reverse of those already considered, any move that prevents their occurrence (and self-financing loans have this effect) would give rise to the same economic developments that have just been discussed in detail.

The Welfare Aspects of Federal Lending

Since the major purpose of a federal loan program is to shift resources from one use to another, it is most important that operational procedures be devised to ensure that the changes involved result in a net gain to society. This is not the place for a detailed analysis of this complex problem, but a brief discussion of welfare tests is needed to complete the evaluation of the role that should be assigned to federal borrowing costs in the administration of federal loan programs. For this purpose, it is essential to distinguish the three major goals of federal lending.

Consider, first, a program that is set up solely to offset imperfections in private credit markets. Since the purpose here is simply to fill a credit gap,[28] the terms offered to borrowers should be the same as those that would prevail in a competitive and efficient private market for the special type of loan involved, if only such a market existed. Direct observation of these terms being impossible, guidance would have to be sought from those private markets that were reasonably competitive, particularly those financing similar economic activities and similar types of borrowers. Having adopted its terms in this way, the federal loan program should become, after its initial period of organization, a profit-making enterprise; and its effectiveness could be tested by comparing its profit rate with those achieved by private lenders. The profit figures should be computed after deduction of administrative expenses and a reasonable allowance for future losses, but before deduction of any interest payments, since these are not real costs but

[28] Credit gaps may exist because of legal or geographical barriers, because of inertia or prejudice on the part of private lenders, or because of the exercise of monopoly power. See James W. McKie, "Credit Gaps and Federal Credit Programs," in Commission on Money and Credit, *Federal Credit Programs* (Prentice-Hall, 1963), pp. 317-53.

rather a distribution of earnings to one group of owners. To compare profits net of interest payments is to use data that are affected not only by economic performance but also by such irrelevant factors as capital structure or the rate of interest at which each enterprise can borrow money.

To suggest a profit test of this kind is not to argue that the federal loan program in question must match the very best kinds of private performance, since the type of business to which it is restricted may well be of the low-profit variety. Nevertheless, a profit rate that consistently fell significantly below private levels would constitute strong evidence that the borrowers being serviced could not in fact find funds in a competitive private credit market. In such a case, federal loans could not be justified simply as offsets to private market imperfections but would need the additional support of one of the two public purposes to be discussed next.

To isolate the second kind of federal loan program, suppose that the borrowers in question do have access to effective private markets, but that the activities for which they are seeking funds confer important social benefits. In the absence of government action, therefore, too few resources would be allocated to those purposes, and the function of federal loans would be to provide the appropriate stimulus. Credit terms offered should obviously be more generous than those available in private markets, but the extent to which they are so must remain a matter of individual judgment unless the social benefits involved can be quantified. If those benefits could, for example, be converted to a specific rate of return on invested capital, the appropriate government lending rate could be easily defined. It would be derived from the basic requirement that the interest payment to the government should equal the interest payment that would be made to a private lender minus the value of the social benefits accruing from the use not only of the loan funds but also of the borrower's own capital. That is,

(1) $rx = ix - sx - sy$, where

r = the appropriate interest rate on government loans,

x = the amount of the loan,

i = the interest rate prevailing on competitive and efficient private credit markets,

s = the social rate of return, and

y = the amount of money put up by the borrower.

Hence:

$$(2) \quad r = i - s(1 + y/x).$$

If the competitive interest rate is 6 percent and the social rate of return on the activities to be financed by federal loans is 2 percent, for example, the government lending rate should be 4 percent on a 100 percent loan and as low as 2 percent on a loan that financed only half of the project's total costs. While an inverse relationship of this sort between the borrower's equity and the rate of interest on his loan is likely to appear most strange to any lender interested only in maximizing profits, the arrangement would tend to bring about the proper allocation of resources, which is the government's principal concern, and at the same time to encourage government borrowers to use their own funds to the maximum extent possible.

Social benefits, of course, are often extremely difficult to measure. When they are, decision makers can only attempt to specify the limits within which the social rate of return may reasonably be thought to lie. Substitution of these two values in equation (2) would then yield the maximum and minimum rates at which the government loans should be offered.

The final type of government loan program to be considered is one set up for a group of borrowers whose low income status entitles them to public support. Low-rate government loans could assist such people to acquire homes and other basic consumer durables and would have some important advantages over straight government gifts granted for the same purpose. With loans, the government would obtain some return on its investment and the borrowers would be given the satisfaction of paying their own way to a large extent, rather than having to rely entirely on public handouts. Here again, the federal lending rate should lie below those prevailing on private markets, but the social benefits arising from income redistribution are too intangible to permit the use of equation (2) and the approach suggested above.

There is, however, a feasible alternative solution. Instead of using the absolute level of private loan charges as its base of reference, the government could take the minimum ratios that private lenders typically require between loan payments and the borrower's income as measures of the maximum mortgage burden that low-income families should be expected to undertake. It could then offer its own loans to these submarginal borrowers on terms that would keep their mortgage payments within reasonable limits, relative to their incomes.[29]

While there are important differences among the welfare tests that are appropriate for different kinds of government loan programs, they all use as a basis of comparison the credit terms that would prevail in well-functioning, competitive private markets. The rate of interest at which the government itself can borrow is not a relevant consideration for this purpose. If the government loans shift resources from some other federal program, the Treasury's borrowing rate is obviously not a variable that would enter into a comparison of the rates of return. If, on the other hand, the shift is from specific private uses, the rates of return of the resources in those areas should set the minimum level of performance for the projects undertaken by government borrowers. Since data on such rates of return may not be readily available, the credit terms that prevail in reasonably efficient private markets financing the same, or similar, kinds of activity are suggested as workable substitutes. By using these terms in the ways suggested above, the government should be able to manage its loan programs so as to raise the general level of economic welfare.

Policy Questions and Issues

Perhaps the best way to summarize the results of this chapter is to apply the analysis presented in it to some of the important policy questions that have been raised concerning federal loan programs. Six questions have been selected for this purpose, one for each of the six major sections of the chapter, and they are answered below in that order.

1. *Can the treatment of loan programs in the federal budget be improved?* Though considerable progress has been made recently in this

[29] For a discussion of some of the problems involved in setting up such a federal loan program in the housing field see George F. Break, "Federal Loan Insurance for Housing," in Commission on Money and Credit, *Federal Credit Agencies* (Prentice-Hall, 1963), pp. 57-62.

respect, the data that summarize federal lending activities still remain widely scattered throughout the budget document (including the Appendix) and as a result fail to have the public impact that they deserve. The reason for setting up a separate federal lending account and for giving it more prominence in summary budget totals is simple. The economic effects of federal loan programs differ in important ways from the effects of other expenditure programs, and a clear picture of federal fiscal operations cannot be obtained as long as lending remains enmeshed in the administrative and cash budgets (and excluded from the national income budget). An example of the confusion that can exist in these circumstances is the belief, apparently widespread, that it is preferable to finance federal expenditures by loan sales rather than by borrowing. The basis of this belief is undoubtedly the fact that, under present budgetary accounting methods, loan sales reduce the size of the deficit, while borrowing does not. As shown below, there are some important differences between the two methods of financing, but their impact on the net wealth of the federal government is not one of them.

My specific recommendation is that a federal lending account be included with the summary tables now given in Part 2 of the Budget,[30] and that it be divided into three main sections:

Federal Lending Account

Expenditures

Receipts

I. *Financial Investment*

Loan Disbursements, D

Loan Purchases, P

Loan Repayments, R

Loan Sales, S

Write-offs, W

Net Financial Investment during Period =
$D + P - R - S - W$ = Change in the Gross Amount of Loans Outstanding.

II. *Real Investment*

Market Value of Real Assets Acquired in Default Proceedings, V

Proceeds from the Sale of Real Assets, X

Change in Agency Inventories of Real Assets $= V - X$.

III. *Profit and Loss Statement*

Administrative Expenses A

Interest and Other Income, Y

Capital Losses on Defaulted Loans, $X - W$

Net Profit (+) or Loss (−) $= Y - A + X - W$.

Net Expenditures of Federal Loan Programs $=$ I − III
$$= D + P + A - R - S - Y - X.$$

Within the three main sections given above, distinctions might also be made between administrative budget and trust fund programs and between national defense and civil programs. In any case, the balances shown by Sections I and III should be carried over into the summary table showing the Consolidated Cash Budget; and when this is done, I recommend that the balance of that Budget be shown both including and excluding the Federal Government's Net Financial Investment for the period in question.

Another useful summary table would compare the government's lending operations with its borrowing from the private sector during the same period. Perhaps the single most valuable classification of the loan securities involved in all of these transactions would be by their terms to maturity. The interested economist could then tell at a glance to what extent the government was borrowing short-term rather than long-term, or selling off loans with short, rather than long, terms still to run.

2. *Do loans have less economic impact per dollar than other kinds of federal expenditures?* The standard answer to this question is an affirmative one. The Cabinet Committee on Federal Credit Programs, for example, stated that "while Government credit programs have varying economic impacts, they normally have less impact per dollar of credit extended than expenditure or tax policy,"[31] and in a 1962 Symposium on Budgetary Concepts, a similar position was taken by the authors of one of the papers.[32] Moreover, the general belief that additional federal expenditures financed by an increase in the public debt can be relied on to have a significant expansionary economic effect implies an affirmative answer to the slightly different question just posed.

In my view the situation is not nearly so simple. Variation in the strength of their economic effects characterizes the components of each of the major categories of government expenditures—loans, transfers,

---

[30] In recent years Table 6 in Pt. 2 has given some information on federal loans, but it is too highly condensed and combines too many unlike elements to be of much use.

[31] *Report to the President on Federal Credit Programs*, p. 38.

[32] Stephen Taylor, Helmut F. Wendel and Daniel H. Brill, "A Synthesis of Federal Accounts," *Review of Economics and Statistics*, Vol. 45 (May 1963), p. 142.

and purchases of goods and services—and no a priori case can be made for the superiority of any one category over any other. Take loans and transfer payments, which are alike in that neither increases aggregate demand directly, but both affect it instead through the reactions of their recipients. Transfers tend to raise private spending by raising disposable incomes, but it should be noted that they leave each recipient free to decide how much of his additional income he will spend and how rapidly. Loans, in contrast, do not make the borrower any better off *immediately*, but they do offer him the prospect of higher future earnings, *if* he spends the loan proceeds wisely. Nor is he encouraged to procrastinate in this activity, because interest charges, and perhaps principal repayments as well, are likely to begin without delay. Because of these pressures and incentives, then, the borrower may well spend his government funds more vigorously and more quickly than the receiver of transfers. That loans have as great expansionary powers as federal purchases of goods and services is more doubtful. Loans are subject to the leakages noted earlier in the chapter, and these are probably, though not necessarily, greater than the leakages (imports and existing assets) that characterize many federal purchases. Theoretical analysis alone, then, establishes no presumption that the economic effects of loans are quantitatively less than the economic effects of other kinds of government expenditures. The question is an empirical one, and the evidence needed to answer it has yet to be presented.

3. *Should federal loans be sold during a period of monetary ease and excess unemployment?* Such a combination of economic conditions presents policy makers with a difficult choice. On the one hand, to sell loans when money markets are easy is to take advantage of the relatively favorable prices that private investors are willing to pay at those times; but on the other, to sell loans when unemployment is excessive is to run a real risk of impeding the economy's recovery to high-level operations. To evaluate that risk is no easy task, but because of the large volume of loan sales made in recent years,[33] it is one well worth attempting.

The basic problem is to specify the fiscal offsets to which loan sales are likely to give rise. While many different combinations are possible,

[33] Discussed in Chap. 3.

for present purposes only two extreme cases are considered: full debt and full expenditure offsets.[34] For the first of these to occur, there must be no relation between the debt sales and either expenditure or tax policies. In these circumstances, debt sales of a given amount would reduce both the reported federal deficit and the outstanding public debt by equal amounts. The whole operation, therefore, would make no change in the volume of financial assets held by the private sector, but by substituting federal loan paper for federal securities, it would increase both the risk and the illiquidity of private investor portfolios. As a result, private borrowers would find funds harder to obtain and would be induced to reduce their expenditures on new output. The more they reacted in this way, of course, the more difficult would the elimination of excess unemployment become.

The second case presupposes such a close connection between debt sales and federal expenditures that a given amount of the former causes a like amount of the latter. Such a combination of fiscal actions would normally be expected to have a net expansionary effect on the economy, though for reasons given in the answer to the preceding question, the size of that net effect might not be great. The important point, however, is that the policy in question does not rank high among the means of eliminating excess unemployment. Additional expenditures financed by the sale of long-term federal debt would be better; expenditures financed by the sale of short-term debt would be better still; and expenditures financed by the creation of new money would be the best of all. We must consider, therefore, in what sense loan sales may be said to permit federal expenditures that otherwise could not have been made.

The answer is that if loan sales do indeed have this power, it is largely because of inadequate accounting procedures and antiquated economic beliefs. Expenditures financed by borrowing have the same effects on the government's net wealth as the identical expenditures financed by the sale of loans, but under present budgetary conventions the former increase the size of the federal deficit, whereas the latter do not. A more realistic method of accounting, such as that recommended above in the answer to the first question, would reveal the es-

---

[34] Tax offsets are also possible but are sufficiently similar to expenditure offsets to be omitted for purposes of discussion.

sential similarity of the two financing procedures. Even in its absence, however, all would still be well except for the widespread tendency to regard a federal deficit as a deterrent to higher government expenditures or to lower taxes even though the economy is operating sufficiently below capacity levels to minimize the danger of inflation. Economic superstitions, such as the balanced budget dogma, have their costs, and one of them is to produce a combination, like the one under discussion here, of expansionary fiscal policies and contractionary monetary policies, that does little to solve the economic problems at which it is directed. Ironically, the ultimate result may be to convert a temporary federal deficit into a chronic budgetary condition.[35]

No one can tell, of course, to what extent federal loan sales simply reduce the size of the public debt or to what extent they induce higher expenditures or lower taxes than otherwise would exist. In neither case, however, does their use during a period of excess unemployment deserve high commendation. At worst they either accentuate or prolong the problem, and at best they represent a sort of fourth-best solution whose effectiveness falls well below what could be accomplished in a more enlightened economic world.

4. *Are direct loan programs good automatic stabilizers?* The appropriate answer to this question would appear to be in the negative. As shown in the fourth section of the chapter, a loan program that kept its terms of credit constant would behave pro- rather than counter-cyclically, since the demand for its services would tend to be greater in prosperity than in recession.[36] While in principle one can conceive of reversing this response mechanism by using formulas that automatically vary federal loan terms in line with changing economic conditions, in practice devising reliable regulators of this sort is likely to prove extremely difficult, if not impossible. A much more promising

[35] For a provocative discussion of the dangers that could arise from widespread adherence to traditional economic beliefs, see J. M. Culbertson, *Full Employment or Stagnation?* For an excellent short discussion of the economic effects of federal deficits and surpluses see *Economic Report of the President . . .* January 1963, pp. 74-83.

[36] In this respect direct loans differ sharply from insured loans. If interest rates on the latter are fixed, lenders find them less attractive when the economy is booming than when it is lagging, and this imparts a built-in countercyclical flexibility to such programs. See George F. Break, *The Economic Impact of Federal Loan Insurance* (National Planning Association, 1961).

alternative is to manage federal loan programs, as already suggested in Chapter 1, with the requirements of economic stabilization in mind.

5. *Should federal loans be financed by the sale of federal debt?* If the analysis of the operation of fiscal offsets to federal lending is correct,[37] debt financing could be assured only by setting up the loan program in question as a separate, self-supporting trust fund with powers to sell its own securities on private capital markets. This kind of fiscal arrangement would be appropriate for a loan program designed primarily to fill a private credit gap. Not only would its operations be subjected to an automatic market test, the desirability of which was noted in the discussion of the welfare aspects of federal lending, but its burdens would fall mainly on private borrowers and might to a large extent simply eliminate the unwarranted benefits those groups previously received from the credit gap. It is true that, as an economic stabilizer, a semi-independent credit agency is less flexible than a fully owned and operated federal program, but in practice this need not be a troublesome drawback.[38]

Other types of federal loan program, however, are best handled within the administrative budget. Their strong public nature means both that a simple market test of efficiency is not appropriate for them and that their burdens should be disseminated in the same way as the burdens of other federal spending programs.

6. *Should Treasury interest costs be included in lending program expenses?* In recent years there has been much argument about *how* this should be done, but little over *whether* it should be done.[39] The implication, of course, is that an affirmative answer to that question can be taken for granted. This analysis, however, points in exactly the opposite direction. The section on fiscal offsets showed that Treasury borrowing costs can be allocated to individual loan programs only in a completely arbitrary way, based on the unwarranted assumption

---

[37] See the third section of this chapter and Chap. 3.

[38] For further details, see the discussion of stabilization policies in Chap. 1 and the analysis of federal secondary mortgage market operations in Chap. 4.

[39] For a systematic analysis of the different imputation procedures that might be used see Arnold H. Diamond, "Interest Rates for Government Lending Programs," *National Tax Journal*, Vol. 13 (December 1960), pp. 320-28, and his recent study for the House Banking and Currency Committee, *A Study of Federal Credit Programs*, Vol. 1 (Government Printing Office, 1964), Chap. 8.

that all federal loans are debt-financed; and the section on economic welfare showed that Treasury borrowing rates are not the rates of return that should be used either in evaluating federal loan programs or in setting the charges they are to make for their loans. Lending policies that are based on federal borrowing costs would, in my view, result in the overexpansion of programs with few social benefits and the undersupport of programs with many. I recommend, therefore, that the present practice of including Treasury interest costs in lending program expenses be discontinued and that they be replaced, for purposes of program evaluation, by the computations suggested above in the section on the welfare aspects of federal lending.

3

Global Trends and Cycles in
Postwar Federal Lending

THIS CHAPTER PRESENTS a quantitative survey of the most prominent features of federal lending between mid-1946 and mid-1963, together with an estimate of the fiscal offsets to which federal loans gave
rise at different times during that period. The treatment is global in
several senses: first, the profile presented is based entirely on net and
gross money flows, no attempt being made to refine these in order to
distinguish one kind of economic effect from another; second, attention is centered on groups of similar loan programs and on major lending agencies, rather than on individual programs; third, cyclical performance is discussed only in terms of complete cycle phases, loan fluctuations within a given phase being left for later discussion. In this
way, it is hoped, the reader can be given a quick, panoramic view of
federal loans and their fiscal offsets during the first seventeen years of
of the postwar period.

The Postwar Period as a Whole,
June 30, 1946—June 30, 1963

For economic analysis, federal direct lending programs may be divided into four broad groups:

1. *Foreign and Defense Lending.* Dominated currently by loan programs administered by the Agency for International Development, the
Export-Import Bank of Washington, and the Defense and Treasury
Departments, this category is distinguished partly by the fact that
many of the loan funds flow abroad, which complicates the economic
analysis considerably, and partly by the fact that national security considerations are frequently an important element in decisions to ap-

prove or refuse loan applications. Loans of this importance, clearly, cannot be expected to contribute in any consistent way to economic stability.

2. *Loans for Marginal Borrowers.* As noted in Chapter 2, the economic effects of loans made to borrowers who lack access to private credit markets differ significantly from the effects of less restricted government loans. Such submarginal loans, however, cannot successfully be isolated from other federal loans. The closest approximation that can be made is to segregate loans granted only to borrowers with limited access to private credit, and this has been done in the present group. The main programs included are those of the Farmers Home, Rural Electrification, and Small Business Administrations.

3. *Unrestricted Loans.* All of the major remaining direct loan programs were set up to fulfill specific purposes and are not restricted to marginal and submarginal borrowers. Included are the secondary market and special assistance functions of the Federal National Mortgage Association, the college housing loans of the Housing and Home Finance Agency, direct home loans of the Veterans Administration, national defense educational loans and, finally, the direct loans made by the Federal Housing and Veterans Administrations under their home loan insurance and guaranty programs, typically to the buyers of houses that have been acquired by the federal government in its default proceedings.

4. *Subsidiary Programs.* The last and least important group involves loans that are made simply because the federal government is engaged in other kinds of spending activity. The Veterans Administration, for example, makes policy loans to holders of government life insurance, both the Public Housing and Urban Renewal Administrations make extensive use of direct and guaranteed loans to provide temporary financing for their programs of aid to local governments, and in selling various kinds of property, the federal government grants loans to the buyers.[1] The subordinate character of all these loans presumably

---

[1] These vendee loans are, of course, similar to the ones made by the Federal Housing Administration (FHA) and Veterans Administration (VA) and included in category 3 above. The separation was made because, unlike loans made to facilitate the sale of surplus government property, FHA-VA vendee loans are part of major federal credit programs and have essentially the same economic effects as VA direct home loans, which form an important part of the unrestricted loan class.

means that if they play a countercyclical role, it is because of changes in the basic spending programs to which they are attracted and not as a result of deliberate manipulation of the loans themselves.

When all major direct lending programs are grouped in the manner just suggested, the pre-eminence of both the foreign and defense and the unrestricted loans is immediately apparent (Table 3-1). Together these two groups disbursed over $35 billion during the period shown, and the net flow of money from the federal government to borrowers was nearly $21 billion. In contrast, the marginal borrower and the subsidiary programs together showed a postwar increase of only $4 billion in the amount of loans outstanding, although their loan disbursements were over $18 billion. Between mid-1946 and mid-1963, seven federal agencies had net loan flows exceeding $1 billion, their standing in order of importance being:

1. Development and Mutual Security Loans (made by the Agency for International Development and its predecessors) ..... $6.1 billion
2. Federal National Mortgage Association ..... 5.0 billion
3. Rural Electrification Administration ..... 3.2 billion
4. United Kingdom Loan (Treasury Department) ..... 3.2 billion
5. Export-Import Bank of Washington ..... 2.7 billion
6. Veterans Administration (direct home and vendee loans) ..... 1.6 billion
7. College Housing Loans (Housing and Home Finance Agency) ..... 1.5 billion

Two other agencies were not far behind, and indeed they would both be in the billion-dollar class if the private loans either insured by or associated with their programs were included in their totals. One is the Farmers Home Administration, which increased its direct and insured loan holdings by $0.9 and $0.5 billion respectively during the postwar period, and the other is the Small Business Administration, which in mid-1963 had jurisdiction over outstanding loans of at least $1.2 billion.[2]

[2] On June 30, 1963, the Farmers Home Administration's Agricultural Credit Insurance Fund had outstanding direct loans of $47 million and insured loans of $474 million. At the same date, outstanding small business loans, made by the Small Business Administration and private banks participating in its program, were $762 million; disaster loans were $84 million; and state and local development company loans were $26 million. In addition, small business investment companies sponsored by the Small Business Administration had loan portfolios of $308 million at the end of September 1962, the last available reporting date. Since small business investment companies have been growing steadily, it may be safely inferred that their holdings at mid-1963 were even larger.

TABLE 3-1. *Postwar Money Flows to Federal Borrowers by Major Program and Group, June 30, 1946—June 30, 1963*

(Billions of dollars)

Group and Lending Program	Postwar Change in Amount of Loans Outstanding (1)	Gross Loan Disbursements (2)	Ratio of Column 1 to Column 2 (3)[a]
Foreign and Defense Programs	$12.1	$19.0	
Development Loans	1.8	1.9	0.95
Mutual Security Loans	4.3	4.9	0.88
Export-Import Bank Loans	2.7	8.0	0.34
United Kingdom Loan	3.2	3.8	0.85
Defense Production Loans	0.1	0.5	0.16
Unrestricted Programs	8.7	16.2[b]	
College Housing Loans	1.5	1.5	0.96
Federal National Mortgage Association Loans	5.0	11.7	0.43
National Defense Educational Loans	0.3	0.3	0.98
Direct Home Loans for Veterans	1.3	2.0	0.63
Federal Housing and Veterans Administration Vendee Loans	0.7	c	c
Marginal-Borrower Programs	3.5	11.6	
Farmers Home Administration Loans	0.9	4.4	0.20
Rural Electrification Loans	2.5	3.7	0.68
Rural Telephone Loans	0.7	0.8	0.92
Small Business Loans	0.6	1.1	0.51
Small Business Investment and Development Company Loans	0.2	0.2	0.92
Reconstruction Finance Corporation	−0.5	1.3	−0.39
Home Owners Loan Corporation	−0.8	0.0	—
Federal Farm Mortgage Corporation	−0.1	0.0	—
Subsidiary Programs	0.4	6.8	
Public Housing Administration	−0.2	4.3	−0.04
Urban Renewal Administration	0.1	0.8	0.17
Veterans Life Insurance Policy Loans	0.5	1.7	0.26
All Groups	24.7	53.6	

Source: App. B.
  [a] Ratios were computed from figures carried to the nearest million dollars. Group totals were obtained in the same way.
  [b] Minimum estimates obtained by substituting net disbursements from column (1) for the missing gross disbursement figures.
  c Not available.

Life Stages and Postwar Trends

During the course of a full and varied lifetime, a government lend-ing program may be expected to go through four principal stages. The infant phase is characterized by little or no lending activity but by an increasing flow of informal inquiries and formal loan applications, by the assembling of a staff of qualified personnel, by the defining of a set of operating procedures, and so forth.

Once a loan program has become firmly established, it is likely to expand rapidly, with the familiar exuberance of youth. During this second stage, loan disbursements typically rise a good deal more rap-idly than principal repayments, especially at the outset, and the in-crease in the amount of loans outstanding is consequently almost as large as the flow of loan disbursements during the same period of time. Youthful loan programs, in other words, tend to have similar net and gross outflows of funds.

As maturity approaches, repayments tend to rise toward the level of disbursements, and the amount of loans outstanding climbs more and more slowly, frequently becoming virtually stationary for extended pe-riods of time. In fact, this last quality may be designated as the distin-guishing characteristic of full maturity, the mark of the program's in-dependence, since repayments of old loans exactly finance disburse-ments on new loans and no calls for money need be made to the Treas-ury.

Full maturity itself may be followed by a period of "easing off," when repayments exceed disbursements and the level of loans out-standing gradually falls. The fourth, and final, stage begins when the loan granting authority of the program is terminated by Congress. Al-though loan disbursements may continue for a brief period, full retire-ment soon sets in as the outstanding portfolio of loans is steadily re-duced, both by the regular inflow of repayments and by the occasional sale of loans to private lenders.

Although this life cycle is apparent in all loan programs, each one has its individual traits. In some cases, the continuing upsurge of dis-bursements may outpace repayments over so long a period as to sug-gest that the program in question has indeed discovered the fountain

CHART 3-1. *Net Loans of Five Youthful Programs*

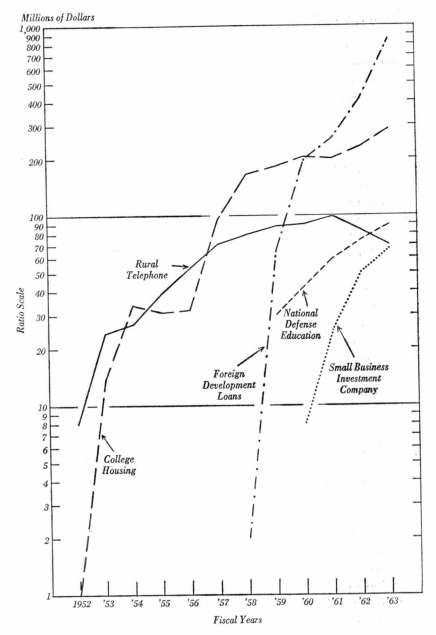

Millions of Dollars

Ratio Scale

Rural Telephone

National Defense Education

Foreign Development Loans

Small Business Investment Company

College Housing

Fiscal Years

CHART 3-2. *Net Loans of Five Mature Programs*

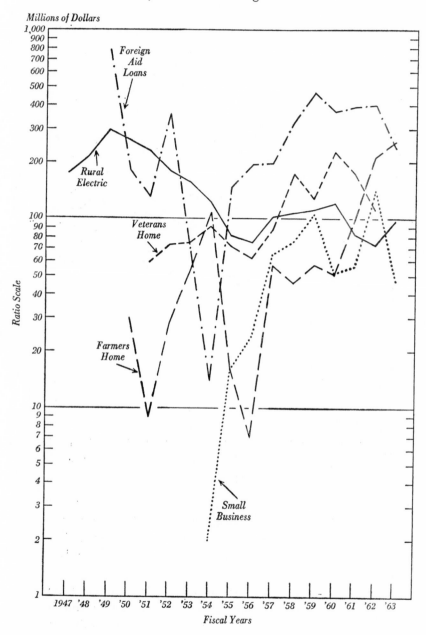

Millions of Dollars

Ratio Scale

Foreign Aid Loans

Rural Electric

Veterans Home

Farmers Home

Small Business

Fiscal Years

1947 '48 '49 '50 '51 '52 '53 '54 '55 '56 '57 '58 '59 '60 '61 '62 '63

CHART 3-3. *Gross Loans of Five Mature Lending Programs*

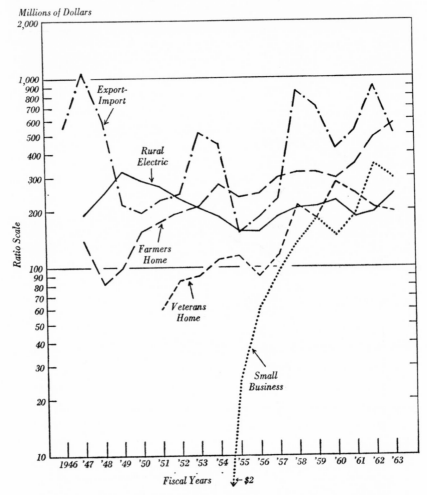

Millions of Dollars

Ratio Scale

Fiscal Years

of youth. In other cases, maturity may be little more than a brief pause between rapid expansion and sharp decline, and in still others the enterprise may settle into an early maturity that promises to last indefinitely. Variations on the four-stage theme, in other words, are numerous.

A glance at the third column of Table 3-1, where the ratio of the postwar change in the amount of loans outstanding to total loan disbursements during the same period is shown for each of the major federal lending programs, will give a quick picture of their different life stages. Youthful programs, like college housing and national defense educational loans, show a net/gross money-flow ratio close to unity; mature programs, like the agricultural loans of the Farmers Home Administration, have a relatively low positive ratio; and retired programs, like those of the Reconstruction Finance Corporation, display a negative ratio. These figures, of course, are averages for the postwar period as a whole and do not imply that each program remained in one stage only for the whole seventeen years. They do, however, provide a helpful guide to a study of postwar trends in the gross and net flows of federal loan funds.

Charts 3-1, 3-2 and 3-3 illustrate the great diversity to be found in these trends. The five youthful lending programs of Chart 3-1 all show rapid initial rates of growth, followed by varying degrees of retardation. Among the mature programs, one may note the highly volatile net loan flows of the Farmers Home Administration and the Agency for International Development (Chart 3-2), as well as the somewhat U-shaped paths traced by the gross disbursements of the Rural Electrification Administration and the Export-Import Bank (Chart 3-3).

Postwar Cycles in Loans and Their Fiscal Offsets

In this section, attention is centered on the individual cyclical phases through which the United States economy has gone since 1946 and on the behavior during these periods of direct federal loans, classified by major group and program. Two quantitative measures form the basis of the discussion: gross loan disbursements, including both advances to private borrowers and purchases of existing loan paper from private lenders; and the change over a given period of time in the amount of federal loans outstanding, equal, for the most part, to the difference between gross loan disbursements and the sum of principal repayments to the government and proceeds from the sale of government loans to private lenders.[3] Taken together, these measures provide a quick picture of the monetary facts as far as federal lending is concerned. Taken in conjunction with other important fiscal and

[3] The write-off of loans in default also reduces the amount outstanding, but this has been a minor factor during the period considered.

monetary developments, some inferences from them can be drawn about the ways in which loan disbursements were probably financed during the postwar period. To these two purposes the present section is devoted.

At the outset, the stages into which postwar business cycles are to be divided must be specified. In one respect, the discussion below is entirely conventional—the dates used for business cycle peaks and troughs are those established by the National Bureau of Economic Research and widely accepted in the profession. These dividing points alone produce four upward and four downward swings in economic activity since the first postwar trough in late 1945. For purposes of stabilization analysis, however, it seems desirable to divide each of the upward swings into two distinct phases—a period of recovery during which the economy was making up the losses of the preceding recession and when a strong case for expansionary fiscal and monetary policies still existed, and a period of expansion during which economic activity rose to new heights and imposed on policy makers a need for caution, and frequently also for the adoption of contractionary policies lest inflationary powers get out of hand.

Given this decision to divide the upswing into two parts, the point of transition from recovery to expansion must be defined. Perhaps the most obvious choice would have been to end the recovery phase as soon as the economy had again attained the level of constant-dollar GNP prevailing at the previous business-cycle peak. According to this test, for example, recovery from the 1960-61 recession was completed in the second quarter of 1961, when GNP reached $443.9 billion (in 1954 dollars), exceeding for the first time the previous peak level of $442.3 billion in the second quarter of 1960. Simple and definite as this solution to the problem would have been, it was rejected in favor of a more complex but, hopefully, more useful one. Specifically, it was decided to extend each peak level of GNP forward in time at some appropriate long-term growth rate and to consider that the recovery phase of the cycle had not ended until actual GNP had risen to intersect that computed trend line. The rate used for this purpose was 3 percent per annum, chosen partly because it is very close to the long-term rates recently established for this country by Edward F. Denison,[4] and

[4] Edward F. Denison, *The Sources of Economic Growth in the United States and the Alternatives Before Us* (Committee for Economic Development, 1962).

partly because it is conservatively low when compared with the rates frequently suggested as targets for policy makers. For present purposes, then, the expansion phase of the cycle does not begin until the economy has recovered from a recession to the level of GNP it would have attained had it simply continued to expand from the peak GNP level at 3 percent per annum.

TABLE 3-2. *Postwar Business Cycle Peaks, Troughs, and Transitions from Recovery to Expansion*

Peak Quarters	Trough Quarters	Transition Quarters	Quarters in Which GNP Attained Its Previous Peak Level
		1946[a]	
1948-IV	1949-IV	1950-II	1950-I
1953-II	1954-III	1955-III	1955-I
1957-III	1958-II	1959-II	1958-IV
1960-II	1961-I	1961-IV	1961-II

Sources: Peak and trough quarters are those of the National Bureau of Economic Research. See, for example, Wilfred Lewis, Jr., *Federal Fiscal Policy in the Postwar Recessions* (Brookings Institution, 1962), p. 4. Transition quarters were computed in the manner described in the text, using official Department of Commerce quarterly estimates of Gross National Product in 1954 dollars and compounding the 3 percent growth rate annually. Quarters in the last column were obtained directly from seasonally adjusted quarterly estimates of GNP in 1954 dollars.

[a] Lack of constant-dollar quarterly estimates of GNP precludes a more precise estimate of this transition date.

Table 3-2 gives the thirteen dates needed to divide postwar business cycles into the four contractions, recoveries, and expansions that form the basis of the following discussion. For purposes of comparison, the quarters in which constant-dollar GNP recovered to its previous peak level are also included, and it will be noted that since 1950 these have preceded the transition dates of this study by two quarters.[5]

The next eight subsections will consider the monetary importance

[5] The transition quarters of this study may also be compared with the terminal recovery quarters used by Wilfred Lewis, Jr., in his study *Federal Fiscal Policy in the Postwar Recessions* (Brookings Institution, 1962). These were defined as the quarters, following recessions, in which the economy returned to high employment. Two of them (1950-II and 1959-II) are identical with those of this study. One of the others (1955-II) precedes by one quarter and the last (1962-II) follows by two quarters the measures of the present analysis. For further details see Lewis, pp. 3-5.

of federal lending during each of the cycle phases identified in Table 3-2. Each subsection contains a two-part tabular summary, the first part dividing direct loan programs into the major groups already discussed and showing for each the net change in the amount of loans outstanding during that particular cycle phase, and the second part ranking the most important individual programs and showing for them both gross and net money flows from the government to the public. Programs undergoing liquidation have been segregated, those in the foreign and defense area being included in the category marked "other" and those in the domestic area being shown separately.

The main features of the eight summary tables are discussed briefly in the accompanying text, with particular attention to other important fiscal developments during the same period and to the probable ways in which the loans were financed. No attempt is made to go into great detail, however, since two comprehensive studies of postwar fiscal policy are already available.[6]

The 1947-1948 Expansion

During the first postwar expansion, federal lending was dominated, not surprisingly, by foreign loans designed to speed recovery and rehabilitation abroad. As Table 3-3 shows, net disbursements on foreign and defense loans during calendar 1947 and 1948 were over $4 billion, three-quarters of this amount going in a single loan to the United Kingdom, and the rest being dispensed by the Export-Import Bank. Domestic programs, in contrast, produced a net money flow of only $750 million during the two-year period. The relative significance of these amounts may be judged by noting that GNP rose by $44 billion in current dollars from the fourth quarter of 1946 to the fourth quarter of 1948.

Fiscal policy during this period was marked both by continuous downward pressure on federal expenditures, exercised jointly by Congress and the administration, and by a persistent congressional attempt to reduce taxes that began in 1946 and culminated with the passage in April of the Revenue Act of 1948 over President Truman's veto.[7] Had

---

[6] A. E. Holmans, *United States Fiscal Policy 1945-1959* (London: Oxford University Press, 1961), and Lewis, *op. cit.*

[7] Holmans, *op. cit.*, pp. 60-73 and 77-96.

TABLE 3-3. *Federal Lending During the 1947-1948 Expansion*

(Billions of dollars)

	Change in the Amount of Loans Outstanding	
Program Group	1947	1948
Foreign and Defense: Major Programs	$0.73	$0.31
Other Programs	2.87	0.16
Total	3.60	0.47
Marginal Borrowers	0.26	0.26
Unrestricted	0.06	0.19
Subsidiary	0.22	0.20
Liquidating, Domestic	−0.22	−0.17
Total	3.92	0.95
Cash surplus or deficit	+5.7	+8.0

	Money Flows During 1947 and 1948	
Major Programs	Net	Gross
United Kingdom Loan	$3.15	$3.15
Export-Import Bank	0.96	1.86
Rural Electrification Administration	0.47	0.51
Federal National Mortgage Association	0.19	0.20
Reconstruction Finance Corporation	0.11	0.36
Total[a]	4.88	6.08

Source: App. B.

[a] In this and the following seven tables detail may not add to the totals shown because of errors of rounding.

federal lending not made its significant contribution to the already excessive degree of liquidity in the economy,[8] inflationary pressures would presumably have been less and budget surpluses larger. Between the first quarters of 1947 and 1949, for example, the GNP price deflator rose by about 10 percent, from 81 to 89 (1954 = 100), and the federal cash surplus averaged $5.5 billion a year between mid-1946

[8] On this aspect of the postwar period, see John G. Gurley, "Liquidity and Financial Institutions in the Postwar Economy," Reprint No. 39 (Brookings Institution, 1960). See also U. S. Joint Economic Committee, *Study of Employment, Growth and Price Levels,* Joint Committee Print, Jan. 25, 1960.

and mid-1949. With fewer federal loans, controls over other types of federal spending might well have been weaker, and the 1948 tax reduction itself might have been made earlier in the period.

The 1948-1950 Recession and Recovery

During this period, federal lending played an important, and on the whole a stabilizing, role. This is particularly evident in the unrestricted and marginal borrower loans, the two groups that are most amenable to countercyclical variation. From a net credit flow of $0.3 billion, at annual rates, during the first half of 1948, these programs expanded to a $0.8 billion rate in the first half of 1949 and still further to a $1.2 billion rate in the second half of that year (Table 3-4). Foreign lending continued, as it had during the preceding expansion, to occupy the dominant position during the first half of 1949, showing a net disbursement rate of $1.5 billion in that period as compared with a $1.0 billion rate in the first half of 1948; but thereafter this group receded rapidly in importance.

The period began under the influence of anti-inflationary monetary and fiscal policies, exemplified by the President's request for a $4 billion increase in taxes made in his Budget message of January 1949. Restrictions on the expenditures of the Reconstruction Finance Corporation were noted in the same message, and an anti-inflationary replacement of government capital in the Federal Home Loan Banks with private funds was suggested.[9] A definite policy shift did not occur until the summer of 1949, when the President withdrew his earlier proposal for a tax increase and replaced it with a recommendation for some relatively minor tax reductions, such as the elimination of federal excises on the transportation of goods. As for expenditures, the main recommendation was for a continuation of existing levels, in spite of a prospective budget deficit, and no need was seen for any significant expansion in public works spending.[10] Congress, in the meantime, was engaged in an economy drive that reduced appropriations moderately and postponed all proposed tax reductions.

In what respects might these developments have been different if

[9] *The Budget of the United States Government for the Fiscal Year Ending June 30, 1950* (Government Printing Office, 1949), pp. M42-M44.
[10] Lewis, *op. cit.*, pp. 112-20.

TABLE 3-4. *Federal Lending During the 1948-1950 Recession and Recovery*

(Billions of dollars)

Program Group	Change in the Amount of Loans Outstanding, Annual Rates		
	First Half 1949	Second Half 1949	First Half 1950
Foreign and Defense	$1.5	$0.2	$0.2
Marginal Borrowers	0.3	0.5	0.4
Unrestricted	0.5	0.7	0.5
Subsidiary	0.0	0.0	0.1
Liquidating, Domestic	−0.3	−0.3	−0.4
Total	2.0	1.1	0.7
Cash surplus or deficit[a]	−3.1	−0.6	−4.5

Major Programs	Net Money Flows		Gross Money Flows	
	1949	First Half 1950 Annual Rate	1949	First Half 1950 Annual Rate
International Cooperation Administration	$0.77	$0.22	$0.77	$0.22
Federal National Mortgage Association	0.63	0.45	0.65[b]	0.51[b]
Rural Electrification Administration	0.30	0.22	0.33	0.25
Export-Import Bank	0.06	0.13	0.18	0.24
Reconstruction Finance Corporation[c]	0.09	0.06	0.27	0.30
Total	1.85	1.08	2.22	1.63

Source: App. B.

[a] Seasonally adjusted figures were taken from U. S. Joint Economic Committee, *Staff Report on Employment, Growth, and Price Levels* (Government Printing Office, 1959), p. 309, and then converted to annual rates.

[b] Mortgage purchases minus mortgage sales.

[c] Liquidating programs excluded.

federal lending had been significantly less? Note first that net loan disbursements were over $1.5 billion in 1949 (Table 3-4) at a time when the budget deficit was increasing from $1.8 billion in fiscal 1949 to $3.1 billion in fiscal 1950. Fewer federal loans, therefore, could have reduced these deficits substantially and, in addition, would probably have made the recession more severe than it was. Just how much more severe is difficult to say since about half of the loans made went to foreign countries and may have exerted their expansionary impact in this country relatively early in the recession, or even before. On the other hand, the second largest loan program, that of the Federal National Mortgage Association, made an important contribution to the 1949-50 housing boom. In these circumstances, it seems most likely that less federal lending would have meant more spending of other kinds. Whether tax policy would have been affected is more debatable, although some excise tax reductions might have been made.

The 1950-1953 Expansion

The importance of the fiscal role played by federal loan programs during the Korean War is well indicated by the fact that their net disbursements during the three fiscal years 1951-53 amounted to $3.4 billion, a figure that exceeded the government's cash surplus for the same period (Table 3-5). Most of the activity was concentrated in the top five loan programs. Of these, two (ICA and EIB) were closely related to the war effort, one (FNMA) gave priority to the financing of construction in critical defense areas, and the other two (REA and VA) were subject to various spending controls designed to restrict their lending to high priority projects.

It is difficult to estimate the extent to which the federal loans of this period were debt-financed. In favor of that type of financing, two important arguments can be cited. The first concerns the Revenue Act of 1950, which was passed quickly in an atmosphere of emergency and was based primarily on expected future levels of federal expenditures. It is very doubtful, therefore, that less federal lending would have affected these 1950 tax increases in any way. Secondly, whereas at other times during the postwar period fewer nondefense loan disbursements might well have meant more nondefense federal spending of other kinds, it is doubtful that such a shift would have occurred during the Korean War. Nor, presumably, would less civilian lending have induced more defense expenditures. If these considerations were the only relevant ones, we could safely conclude that federal loans in 1950-53 were debt-financed, since they induced neither higher taxes nor lower expenditures than otherwise would have existed.

In opposition to this conclusion, however, one caveat should be en-

TABLE 3-5. *Federal Lending During the 1950-1953 Expansion*

(Billions of dollars)

| | Change in the Amount of Loans Outstanding | | | |
Program Group	Fiscal 1951	Fiscal 1952	Fiscal 1953	Total
Foreign and Defense	$0.2	$0.5	$0.3	$1.0
Marginal Borrowers	0.2	0.1	0.2	0.5
Unrestricted	0.6	0.6	0.5	1.7
Subsidiary	0.2	0.1	0.0	0.3
Liquidating, Domestic	−0.1	−0.1	−0.0	−0.2
Total	1.1	1.3	1.0	3.4
Cash surplus or deficit	+7.6	−0.0	−5.3	+2.3

| | Money Flows, Fiscal 1951–1953 | |
Major Programs	Net	Gross
Federal National Mortgage Association	$1.44	$1.68[a]
Rural Electrification Administration	0.60	0.74
International Cooperation Administration	0.56	0.57
Export-Import Bank	0.37	0.99
Veterans Administration Direct Housing Loans	0.21	0.23
Total	3.18	4.21

Source: App. B.

[a] Mortgage purchases minus mortgage sales.

tered. A second, substantial round of tax increases was recommended in early 1951, based largely on the size of the federal deficits then expected, but these proposals encountered a very different reception from those of 1950. Prolonged hearings were held in Congress, and, as a result of widespread opposition and resistance, the final tax increases fell substantially short of the original recommendations.[11] Had federal lending at the time been less, inflationary pressures would have been weakened and budget deficits decreased. It is possible that these changes would have reduced the amount of the 1951 tax increases,

[11] Holmans, *op. cit.*, pp. 151-82.

partly because the President might have recommended less of an increase and partly because congressional opposition to higher taxes might have been strengthened. After late 1951, therefore, the possibility that federal loans were tax-financed cannot be lightly dismissed.

As already noted, many of the federal loans made in 1950-53 were strongly defense-oriented. In the absence of such disbursements, might it not have been necessary to make additional nonloan expenditures for the same purpose? If so, the lending programs in question may be said to have been expenditure-financed. Unlike other types of public spending, however, loans do result in future reverse money flows from the private sector to the government. Wartime loans, in other words, may have important implications for postwar stabilization policy.

The 1953-1955 Recession and Recovery

Less important during this period than in any of the other three postwar recessions and recoveries, federal lending played a predominantly procyclical role. Direct loans outstanding, as Table 3-6 shows, fell off by $0.3 billion in recession-dominated fiscal 1954 and then rose by $0.6 billion in fiscal 1955. In each case most of the activity took place relatively late in the fiscal year, direct federal loans outstanding falling at an annual rate of $1.1 billion during the first half of calendar 1954, when administrative concern over the recession was at its peak, and rising at an annual rate of $0.9 billion during the first half of calendar 1955, when an early return to high output and employment was expected.

Federal fiscal policies in 1953-55 were aimed primarily at the long-run goal of the Eisenhower Administration to reduce both expenditures and tax rates and to do so in such a way as to eliminate the existing budget deficit. Since the net economic impact of such actions was likely to be deflationary, a potential conflict with short-run stabilization objectives arose as soon as the recession began in the summer of 1953. Prepared during the fall of that year, the first Eisenhower budget proposed a $5.3 billion cut in expenditures for fiscal 1955 and a $5.0 billion reduction in taxes, most of which was to occur automatically at the beginning of 1954.[12] As a result the administrative deficit was to fall

---

[12] *The Budget of the United States Government for the Fiscal Year Ending June 30, 1955* (Government Printing Office, 1954), pp. M7-M8.

below $3 billion, and the cash budget was to show the first surplus since early in the Korean War. Further contraction was the order of the day for all federal loan programs except those connected with urban renewal activities, which were to be broadened in scope, and a new program of interest-free planning loans was recommended to stimulate the establishment of a shelf of state and local public works that could quickly be activated if the recession got worse. Nearly halfway through the recession, then, the outlook was for a moderately deflationary federal budget.

As unemployment continued to increase—a peak of 6.1 percent of the labor force was reached in September 1954—two expansionary fiscal actions altered the picture somewhat. One was the reduction in excise tax rates passed by Congress and signed by the President in March, involving an annual revenue loss of $1 billion that had not

TABLE 3-6. *Federal Lending During the 1953-1955 Recession and Recovery*

(Billions of dollars)

Program Group	Change in the Amount of Loans Outstanding	
	Fiscal 1954	Fiscal 1955
Foreign and Defense	$0.11	$0.13
Marginal Borrowers	0.25	0.15
Unrestricted	−0.05	0.27
Subsidiary	−0.38	−0.04
Liquidating, Domestic	−0.26	0.07
Total	−0.33	0.58
Cash surplus or deficit	−0.23	−2.70

	Net Money Flows		Gross Money Flows	
Major Programs	1954	1955	1954	1955
Rural Electrification Administration	$0.15	$0.12	$0.21	$0.20
Veterans Administration	0.10	0.08	0.11	0.12
International Cooperation Administration	0.01	0.15	0.01	0.15
Export-Import Bank	0.16	−0.03	0.44	0.15
Federal National Mortgage Association	−0.20	0.25	−0.08[a]	0.41[a]

Source: App. B.

[a] Mortgage purchases minus mortgage sales.

been proposed in the January Budget, and the other was the cabinet decision of May 14 to accelerate the making of certain fiscal 1955 expenditures, shifting them from the second to the first half of that year in an attempt to end the recession.[13] As things turned out, most of the impact of the expenditure speed-up occurred after the recovery was well under way, in the last quarter of 1954 and the first quarter of 1955.[14] Two loan programs were directly involved—farm housing loans of the Farmers Home Administration and REA electric and telephone loans—but it is difficult to detect any pronounced effect on their credit flows.[15] Nor was the downward pressure on low-priority expenditures lessened, while, of course, the short-run increase in essential spending was to be reversed at a later stage, hopefully within fiscal 1955 itself. The actions taken, in other words, did not represent any important sacrifice of long-run fiscal goals.

By the end of 1954, it was widely recognized that economic expansion was once more under way, and when the new Budget was submitted in January, the unemployment rate had already fallen below 5 percent. Continued downward pressure on expenditures, together with stable tax rates, was proposed, and note was taken of the hopeful prospects of eliminating the deficit. Federal lending programs fared somewhat better than they had in the previous year.[16] Modest increases in REA loans were recommended; the urban renewal program continued to be pushed; Congress was asked to extend the lives of the Small Business Administration and the Veterans Administration direct home loan program, both scheduled to expire in mid-1955; and in March a special message to Congress on foreign aid proposed that loans be substituted for grants to the maximum extent possible. Downward pressure on other types of direct loans continued, however, the general aim being to substitute private for government credit. In part, this shift was to be accomplished by the sale of existing government loans to private lenders, as was done later in the year by the RFC, and by increases in federal interest rates, as in the case of the

---

[13] Lewis, *op. cit.*, pp. 165-70.

[14] *Ibid.*, pp. 177-82.

[15] See Apps. A and B.

[16] *The Budget of the United States Government for the Fiscal Year Ending June 30, 1956* (Government Printing Office, 1955), pp. M61 and M75-M78.

college housing program, but the most important recommendation was that direct loans be replaced by federally insured private loans. The attractions of this last policy were that it would reduce the federal deficit and might well do so without exerting a deflationary impact on the economic system.[17]

In 1953-54 the fiscal offsets to federal lending appear to have undergone a definite change. During 1953 it is doubtful that lending affected either taxes or nonloan expenditures, and hence it is most probable that loan disbursements in that year were debt-financed. This conclusion rests on two considerations. Not only were direct loans relatively unimportant during this period, perhaps sufficiently so that even policy makers intent on short-run economic stabilization would have disregarded them, but in 1953 policy makers were more concerned with the longer-run objectives of converting the federal government to a peacetime basis and reducing it substantially in size, and the effects of the actions taken had not yet become clearly discernible.[18]

The following year, however, presents a different picture. Federal loans increased in importance, particularly during the first half of 1954, when they declined at an annual rate of $1.1 billion; and federal fiscal actions became increasingly influenced by the existence of the recession and of the federal deficit. Several of the changes made might have been different had direct loan disbursements been smaller than they in fact were.[19] The expenditure speed-up inaugurated in May, for example, might have been expanded, and some increase might have been made in the tax reductions (estimated at $1.4 billion in fiscal 1955) resulting from the structural reforms enacted in the

[17] Undoubtedly it was assumed that fewer direct loans would simply reduce the amount of federal debt outstanding (rather than reducing taxes or increasing nonloan expenditures). Private lenders, therefore, might be induced to shift their funds from the purchase of federal securities to the making of federally insured loans, and private borrowers would receive these loans rather than direct federal credit. As indicated below, however, the situation in 1954 was not nearly so clear-cut, and there is a good chance that fewer direct loans would, in fact, have meant either lower taxes or higher nonloan expenditures. In that case, the net effect of the whole operation might well have been expansionary.

[18] Holmans, op. cit., pp. 199-210, 214-19, and Lewis, op. cit., pp. 133-42.

[19] With smaller loan disbursements, direct loans outstanding would have fallen more than they did, the recession would have been intensified, and the budget deficit would probably have been reduced.

summer under the Internal Revenue Code of 1954. Even the excise tax reductions enacted in March might have been larger, but the fact that rates were lowered to a general 10 percent level argues against this possibility.

Thereafter, fiscal policy returned to its long-run objectives, and the question to be answered is whether federal lending either intensified downward pressures on other expenditures or postponed the hoped-for reductions in tax rates. This, however, is a problem for the next section.

The 1955-1957 Expansion

During the first half of the investment boom of 1955-57, the amount of direct federal loans outstanding increased by only $0.3 billion, compared to $0.6 billion in fiscal 1955. But in fiscal 1957 the rise jumped to $1.3 billion. As a result, the average annual increase in amounts outstanding for the expansion period as a whole was $0.8 billion (Table 3-7), substantially above the $0.1 billion average for the preceding recession and recovery. While the foreign and defense group shifted from a positive to a negative net money flow, unrestricted loan programs expanded greatly, largely as a result of FNMA mortgage purchases. Four other lending agencies made gross disbursements averaging $0.2 billion or more during the expansion, but two of these, the Export-Import Bank and the Farmers Home Administration, had virtually no net disbursements (Table 3-7).

Fiscal policy during this period combined expenditure restraint with the maintenance of existing tax rates, while the cash budget as a whole moved from a deficit of −$2.7 billion in fiscal 1955 to surpluses in 1956 and 1957 averaging $3.3 billion a year. The budget for 1956 proposed a cut in expenditures and held out some hope for a tax reduction, but neither of these changes materialized. Expenditures rose both in that year and in the next, and annual one-year extensions of the "temporary" wartime excise and corporate tax rates were made on schedule each April first.

There was, however, considerable talk of tax relief whenever economic and budget conditions permitted—i.e. when prices stopped rising and a sufficiently large budget surplus was in sight—and a number

TABLE 3-7. *Federal Lending During the 1955-1957 Expansion*

(Billions of dollars)

Program Group	Average Annual Change in Amount of Loans Outstanding, Fiscal 1956 and 1957
Foreign and Defense: Major Programs	$0.18
Others	−0.29
Total	−0.11
Marginal Borrowers	0.23
Unrestricted	0.84
Subsidiary	0.05
Liquidating, Domestic	−0.20
Total	0.81
Cash surplus	3.32

Major Programs	Net Money Flows, Average Annual Rate	Gross Money Flows, Average Annual Rate
Federal National Mortgage Association	$0.63	$0.64[a]
International Cooperation Administration	0.20	0.20
Rural Electrification Administration	0.15	0.23
Veterans Administration Direct Housing Loans	0.08	0.10
College Housing Loans	0.06	0.07
Farmers Home Administration	0.03	0.27
Export-Import Bank	−0.03	0.21
Total	1.12	1.72

Source: App. B.

[a] Mortgage purchases minus mortgage sales.

of tax reform laws involving minor losses of revenue were passed.[20] As it happened, expected budget surpluses were largest in late 1956 and early 1957, when federal loans were undergoing their most rapid expansion of the period. In the absence of this expansion, inflationary pressures in the private sector might have been less,[21] and the cash

[20] For details see the *Annual Report of the Secretary of the Treasury on the State of the Finances for the Fiscal Year Ended June 30, 1955* and *ibid., 1956* (Government Printing Office, 1956 and 1957).

[21] Between the second quarters of 1956 and 1957, for example, the GNP price deflator rose from 103.6 to 107.8 (1954 = 100).

surplus would have been pushed close to $5 billion a year. In such circumstances, a tax cut might well have materialized.

During fiscal 1956, federal loans were in all likelihood either expenditure- or debt-financed, and their relative unimportance in that year is a strong argument in favor of the latter alternative. After mid-1956, however, the probabilities increase considerably for some expenditure offset to the rapidly rising loan disbursements. In particular, one may note the struggle over the Budget submitted in January 1957, the administration's vacillation over whether the original expenditure estimates should or should not be cut, and the efforts of both Congress and the administration to reduce future spending levels.[22] Alternatively, as just indicated, there is a good chance that federal lending played an important role in preventing both the long-awaited general tax reduction and the enactment of structural reforms involving significant revenue losses.[23]

The 1957-1959 Recession and Recovery

During fiscal 1958, which witnessed both the beginning of the recession in July and its ending in April, federal direct loans outstanding rose by $1.5 billion (Table 3-8), an increase greater than any annual increase achieved during the preceding two periods of economic expansion and $0.2 billion above the 1957 rise. Recovery from the recession lasted about a year, from the second quarter of 1958 to the second quarter of 1959, and during this period net loan disbursements reached a record level of nearly $2.5 billion. As Table 3-8 shows, foreign and defense loans predominated during the recession, expanded still more in fiscal 1959, but were exceeded in that year by FNMA mortgage operations. The other three major programs—REA, VA, and college housing loans—maintained a stable net money flow of $0.5 billion a year, which was more than 70 percent above their fiscal 1956-57 level. In general, then, federal lending exerted its strongest mon-

[22] During 1957, Congress, for the first time since 1953, reduced spending authority below the level recommended in the Budget, and the administration was simultaneously taking steps to reduce defense spending. Cf. Lewis, op. cit., pp. 188-96.

[23] Among the reform proposals that were successfully opposed by the Treasury were bills to liberalize the tax treatment of retirement provisions made by self-employed people, to extend foreign tax credit carryovers, and to reduce taxes on contributions to the railroad retirement fund.

TABLE 3-8. *Federal Lending During the 1957-1959 Recession and Recovery*

(Billions of dollars)

Program Group	Change in the Amount of Loans Outstanding	
	Fiscal 1958	Fiscal 1959
Foreign and Defense: Major Programs	$0.75	$0.98
Other Programs	−0.21	−0.36
Total	0.54	0.62
Marginal Borrowers	0.33	0.38
Unrestricted	0.71	1.64
Subsidiary	0.05	0.01
Liquidating, Domestic	−0.16	−0.21
Total	1.47	2.44
Cash Deficit	−1.58	−13.09

	Net Money Flows		Gross Money Flows	
Major Programs	1958	1959	1958	1959
Federal National Mortgage Association	0.28	1.23	0.33[a]	1.29[a]
Export-Import Bank	0.41	0.47	0.85	0.71
International Cooperation Administration[b]	0.33	0.53	0.37	0.60
Rural Electrification Administration	0.19	0.20	0.29	0.30
College Housing Loans	0.16	0.18	0.17	0.18
Veterans Administration Direct Housing Loans	0.17	0.13	0.21	0.18
Total	1.54	2.74	2.22	3.26

Source: App. B.

[a] Mortgage purchases minus mortgage sales.

[b] Includes the Development Loan Fund.

etary impact during the last part of the period of high unemployment.

Federal loans were by no means unique in reacting slowly to the expansionary needs created by the recession. The Budget submitted to Congress in early 1958, some six months after the beginning of economic contraction, projected only limited expansion in defense spending and recommended both curtailment of civilian expenditures and the maintenance of existing tax rates. Small cash surpluses were foreseen in both fiscal 1958 and fiscal 1959. Direct loans, then expected to rise more rapidly by mid-1958 than they in fact did,[24] were to be replaced by guaranteed private loans "to the maximum feasible extent,"[25] and interest rate increases were recommended for a number of programs. Fiscal actions designed to counteract the recession were not inaugurated until early March, only a month before the trough was reached.[26] There then ensued, however, a rather extensive series of administrative and legislative steps to expand or accelerate expenditures. Operational speed-ups, increased funds, and more liberal credit terms were provided for a number of loan programs, as will be shown later. On the tax side, refunds of 1957 overpayments were accelerated, and in late June excise tax reductions with a fiscal 1959 revenue impact of −$390 million were made part of the annual tax-extension bill, in spite of Presidential opposition. According to Lewis, mid-July marked the end, for all practical purposes, of antirecession fiscal actions.[27]

The most likely fiscal impact of federal loans between mid-1957 and mid-1958 appears to have been on other government expenditures. Fewer loans during the early part of this period might well have eased existing spending restrictions, particularly those on nondefense programs, and fewer loans later would presumably have increased both the intensity of the recession and the expected size of the budgetary surplus. As a result, antirecession expenditure expansions might have been inaugurated before March 1958, and once begun, might have been carried further than they were. Although tax cuts were not part of the administration's 1958 fiscal policy, there is some chance that fewer loan disbursements would have altered this position, and perhaps a greater chance that Congress would have been induced to

[24] The Special Credit Analysis in the Budget submitted in January 1958 predicted that direct loans outstanding would increase by $2.4 billion between mid-1957 and mid-1958, but the actual rise over that period turned out to be only $1.6 billion. These computations exclude the Commodity Credit Corporation because of the special character of its direct loan operations, but they include the FNMA Secondary Market Operations Trust Fund, which is segregated in the Budget from other loan programs. See *The Budget of the United States Government for the Fiscal Year Ending June 30, 1959* (Government Printing Office, 1958), pp. 907-17.

[25] *Ibid.*, p. M30.

[26] Lewis, *op. cit.*, p. 208.

[27] *Ibid.*, p. 218.

enact larger revenue reductions than it in fact did when the extension of wartime excise and corporate tax rates came up in late June.

During the remainder of 1958, federal fiscal policy became increasingly restrictive, partly in response to the large deficit anticipated for fiscal 1959. Since direct loans accounted for almost 20 percent of the deficit finally shown by the administrative budget,[28] their absence might have mitigated somewhat the administration's drive to hold down expenditures, both then and in the following year.

The 1959-1960 Expansion

The short expansion that began in the second quarter of 1959 and ended a year later is distinguished, among other things, by its lack of vigor (GNP in constant dollars grew less than 3 percent) and by the fact that in no quarter did the unemployment rate fall below 5 percent. For many, these characteristics would justify a less contractionary fiscal policy than was in fact pursued. Others, however, might take the opposite view, basing it primarily on the continued, slow upward drift of prices. The GNP price deflator, for example, rose from 112.4 at the beginning to 114.2 at the end (1954 = 100).

Whatever the stabilization needs of the period, federal loans during fiscal 1960[29] rose by $2.34 billion (Table 3-9), an increase only slightly less than that of the preceding year. Few changes occurred in the top six loan programs. As in the previous year FNMA predominated, with foreign loans in second place in spite of the important decline in Export-Import Bank operations. Each of the remaining programs expanded somewhat, the greatest increase of the three being shown by VA direct housing loans.

Federal expenditures continued to be under strong downward pressures during the expansion, and the Budget for the period, submitted to Congress in January 1959, proposed not only the postponement of all scheduled tax rate reductions but also gasoline tax and postal rate increases designed to expand federal receipts by over $1 billion a year.[30]

---

[28] Net expenditures for federal loan programs in fiscal 1959 were $2.3 billion, whereas the administrative and cash deficits were $12.4 and $13.1 billion respectively.

[29] The expansion did not coincide exactly with this year, but the correspondence is close enough for our purposes at this point.

[30] *The Budget of the United States Government for the Fiscal Year Ending June 30, 1960* (Government Printing Office, 1959), p. M21.

TABLE 3-9. *Federal Lending During the 1959-1960 Expansion*

(Billions of dollars)

Program Group	Change in the Amount of Loans Outstanding During Fiscal 1960
Foreign and Defense: Major Programs	$0.35
Other Programs	−0.20
Total	0.14
Marginal Borrowers	0.34
Unrestricted	2.12
Subsidiary	0.07
Liquidating, Domestic	−0.34
Total	2.34
Cash surplus	0.75

Major Programs	Money Flows During Fiscal 1960	
	Net	Gross
Federal National Mortgage Association	$1.51	$1.61[a]
International Cooperation Administration and Development Loan Fund	0.56	0.60
Veterans Administration Direct Housing Loans	0.23	0.28
Rural Electrification Administration	0.21	0.32
College Housing Loans	0.20	0.21
Export-Import Bank	−0.23	0.42
Total	2.49	3.44

Source: App. B.

[a] Mortgage purchases minus mortgage sales.

In the event, federal expenditures increased by nearly $1.5 billion (national income basis) between the second quarters of 1959 and 1960, but receipts increased by more than $5 billion during the same period, partly as a result of the $0.7 billion increase in gasoline taxes initiated in October 1959 and the $2 billion increase in social security payroll taxes made on schedule at the beginning of 1960. The fact that both of these increases applied to taxes earmarked for specific expenditure programs, the larger of the two occurring automatically, reduces substantially the probability that they would not have been made, or would have been made in smaller amounts, had federal lending during

1959-60 been less vigorous. On the other hand, federal loans did have important economic and budgetary effects at this time, and their absence might well have weakened economy sentiments sufficiently to allow other types of expenditures to expand instead.

The 1960-1962 Recession and Recovery

In fiscal 1961, which included almost all of the recession as well as the first four months of the subsequent recovery, federal loans outstanding continued to rise but only by $0.8 billion, compared to $2.3 billion in 1960 (Tables 3-9 and 3-10). The slowdown was more than eliminated, however, by the $2.6 billion increase in fiscal 1962. Among the programs that continued to expand in spite of the recession, the most notable were foreign loans (both AID and EIB), loans for marginal borrowers, and college housing loans.

One of the most interesting features of the fiscal policies pursued in 1961 by the Kennedy Administration is their similarity to the course of action taken by the Republicans during the preceding recession and recovery. As in 1957-58, attention was concentrated heavily on the expenditure side of the budget, some spending programs, such as the construction of interstate highways, being accelerated, while others, notably national defense, were expanded in size. Once again, as will be shown later, a number of loan programs were provided with additional funds, and in some cases lending terms were liberalized. Tax reductions, in contrast, were relegated to the second line of defense by the Samuelson task force,[31] and no action of this kind was taken until October 1961, when the depreciation schedules for textile machinery under the income tax were liberalized, too late to have a significant impact before the end of the recovery period. In the meantime, at mid-year, scheduled reductions in corporate and excise tax rates had been postponed, and the Federal-Aid Highway Act of 1961 had imposed additional taxes on the truck and rubber industries designed to yield $150 million a year.[32] Still larger increases (nearly $1 billion a

---

[31] Reprinted in *New York Times*, Jan. 6, 1961. The President's tax message of April 20, 1961, proposed a set of reforms that would have involved no loss of revenue. See *Annual Report of the Secretary of the Treasury on the State of the Finances for Fiscal Year Ended June 30, 1961* (Government Printing Office, 1962), pp. 303-13.

[32] 75 Stat. 193 (1961) and 75 Stat. 122 (1961).

TABLE 3-10. *Federal Lending During the 1960-1962 Recession and Recovery*

(Billions of dollars)

Program Group	Change in the Amount of Loans Outstanding	
	Fiscal 1961	Fiscal 1962
Foreign and Defense: Major Programs	$0.74	$1.01
Other Programs	−0.83	−0.04
Total	−0.09	0.98
Marginal Borrowers	0.38	0.60
Unrestricted	0.63	1.08
Subsidiary	0.06	0.17
Liquidating, Domestic	−0.15	−0.20
Total	0.83	2.63
Cash Deficit	−2.30	−5.80

Major Programs[a]	Net Money Flows		Gross Money Flows	
	1961	1962	1961	1962
Agency for International Development	$0.64	$0.81	$0.73	$1.04
Federal National Mortgage Association	0.06	0.43	0.24[b]	0.63[b]
College Housing Loans	0.20	0.23	0.21	0.25
Rural Electrification Administration	0.18	0.16	0.29	0.29
Export-Import Bank	0.14	0.20	0.53	0.90
Small Business Administration	0.09	0.21	0.19	0.35
Farmers Home Administration	0.10	0.20	0.37[c]	0.59[c]
Veterans Administration Direct Housing Loans	0.17	0.11	0.24	0.21
Total	1.58	2.35	2.80	4.26

Source: App. B.
[a] Ranked according to the total 1961-62 net money flow.
[b] Mortgage purchases minus mortgage sales.
[c] Includes Agricultural Credit Insurance Fund.

year) were enacted for both unemployment and social security payroll taxes, but the starting date was set forward to January 1, 1962.[33]

Had fewer federal loans been made during 1960 and 1961 than were

[33] The Temporary Extended Unemployment Compensation Act of 1961, 75 Stat. 8 (1961) and the Social Security Amendments of 1961, 75 Stat. 131 (1961).

TABLE 3-11. *Sales of Federal Loans to Private Investors, by Agency, Program, and Fiscal Year*[a]

(Millions of dollars)

Agency and Program	Fiscal Year		
	1962	1963	1965[b]
Export-Import Bank			
Sale of portfolio certificates with recourse	$300	$250	$700
Loan sales with recourse	—	5	124
Loan sales without recourse	39	81	84
Federal National Mortgage Association			
Special assistance functions	79	293	348
Management and liquidation functions	10	14	167
Proposed pool participations	—	—	200
Veterans Administration			
Direct housing loans	19	181	200
Vendee home loans	29	279	263
Proposed pool participations	—	—	100
Other agencies	—	39	87
Total	476	1,142	2,274

Sources: *The Budget of the United States Government, Fiscal Year Ending June 30, 1964, Appendix,* pp. 761-63, 803-05 and 828; *The Budget of the United States Government, Fiscal Year Ending June 30, 1965,* p. 379 and *Appendix,* p. 811.

[a] Tabulations exclude sales by programs such as FNMA's secondary market fund or the Farmers Home Administration's loan insuring fund that sell loans as a regular part of their operations.

[b] Estimated.

in fact extended, other spending programs might well have been expanded more vigorously, particularly during the spring and summer of 1961, but it is doubtful that tax policy during the period would have been affected. That a contraction of direct lending during fiscal 1961 could have had an important fiscal and economic impact is indicated by the fact that the top eight programs had net disbursements of $1.6 billion (Table 3-10), nearly 70 percent of the 1961 cash deficit. In the next year the monetary impact of these programs was still greater, although they contributed only 40 percent of the 1962 cash deficit of —$5.8 billion. By late 1961 increasing attention was being given to tax reform and tax reduction, and hence the probabilities for some tax off-sets to expanding direct loans were increasing.

At the same time, there was a renewal of interest in the sale of federal loans, and during fiscal 1962 a balance of nearly $500 million was transferred in this way to the private sector. The next year sales more than doubled, and a further doubling was planned in the 1965 Budget (Table 3-11). Three federal agencies—the Export-Import Bank, the Federal National Mortgage Association and the Veterans Administration—carried out most of the transactions, and use was made of both repurchase agreements and other guaranty contracts to make the loan paper more attractive to private lenders. The 1965 Budget also indicated that the Johnson administration would propose legislation permitting the sale of participations in pooled federal holdings of mortgages, a device that was used by the Reconstruction Finance Corporation to accelerate its liquidation in 1953-54.[34]

The immediate object of these rather substantial loan sales was to reduce the size of the reported federal deficit and to keep the public debt within its legislative ceiling. Had this been the only result achieved, the policy would have tightened private money markets at a time when high unemployment called for the opposite kind of action. However, the loan sales did permit the Kennedy Administration to increase federal expenditures by larger amounts than would otherwise have been possible. This is another example, working now in the opposite direction, of an expenditure-offset to federal lending operations. Although, during a period of underemployment, the combination of expenditures and loan sales is preferable to loan sales alone, it is not (as argued in Chapter 2) the most appropriate fiscal policy in the circumstances.

Summary

Judged on the basis of their net money flows alone, federal loan programs behaved countercyclically during three of the four recessions discussed above. The largest increases in the amount of direct loans outstanding occurred in calendar 1949 and fiscal 1958 ($1.6 and $1.5 billion respectively); fiscal 1961 showed an increase only half as great ($0.8 billion), and fiscal 1954 had a procyclical decline of −$0.3 billion. One might argue, however, that for stabilization purposes federal

[34] Discussed in Chap. 4 below.

lending should expand during a recession more rapidly than it increased during the preceding business cycle expansion. By this more severe test, federal loans behaved countercyclically only in calendar 1949 and fiscal 1958, whereas in the other two recession years they fell off significantly from their previous-year performance (Table 3-12).

Some suggestion of a trend appears in the four postwar fiscal years that were dominated by economic recovery. Although in 1950 and 1955 direct loans outstanding rose by only $0.9 and $0.6 billion respectively, in 1959 they increased by $2.4 billion and in 1962 by $2.6 billion. Lend-

TABLE 3-12. *Annual Changes in the Amount of Direct Federal Loans Outstanding*

(Billions of dollars)

Calendar Year	Dominant Business Cycle Phase[a]	All Direct Loan Programs
1947	E	$3.9
1948	E	0.9
1949	C	1.6
Fiscal Year		
1950	R	0.9
1951	E	1.1
1952	E	1.3
1953	E	1.0
1954	C	−0.3
1955	R	0.6
1956	E	0.3
1957	E	1.3
1958	C	1.5
1959	R	2.4
1960	E	2.3
1961	C	0.8
1962	R	2.6

Source: Tables 3-3 through 3-10.
[a] E = expansion, C = contraction, and R = recovery.

ing operations, in other words, were expansionary during all four recoveries and more so at the end than at the beginning. Finally, it is
interesting to note that the average net money flow to the private sector during the four recoveries ($1.7 billion a year) was slightly larger
than the average flow during the eight years of economic expansion
($1.5 billion a year) and significantly above the $0.9 billion average
flow during the four recession years.

As for the fiscal offsets that federal lending may have generated during the postwar period, the preceding discussion indicated on the one
hand some of the difficulties involved in answering this question and
attempted on the other to make as many specific selections as seemed
reasonable. These are brought together in the listing below, admittedly
at the risk of endowing them with more certainty than they deserve.
I stress, therefore, that the choice of one method of financing—reductions in other types of federal expenditures, tax increases, or debt
sales—means only that I view its use as being more likely than the use
of either of the other two. Double choices, with the order of preference
indicated by the numbers 1 and 2, have been used when no one possibility seemed to stand out above the others, and inevitably some periods have had to be omitted because no choice at all seemed feasible.
For what it is worth, then, the list is as follows:

Calendar Year	Fiscal Year	Most Probable Fiscal Offset to Federal Loans		
		Expenditures	Taxes	Debt Sales
1947		1	2	
1948		1	2	
1949		1		
	1950	1		
1951	1951			1
1952			2	1
1953				1
1954		1	1	
	1956	2		1
	1957	1	1	
	1958	1		
	1959	1	2	
	1960	1		
	1961	1		
	1962	1	2	

If these estimates are realistic, postwar federal loans had some re-strictive impact on other types of federal expenditures in every year except those dominated by the Korean War. Upward pressures may also have been exerted on tax rates, notably in 1954 and 1957. Under peacetime conditions debt sales clearly run a poor third though their quantitative importance may be greater than is suggested by the pre-ceding tabulation. Be that as it may, the evidence presented rejects the common assumption that federal loans are always, and exclusively, financed by debt sales.

To argue that loan disbursements have frequently been made at the expense of other types of federal spending is to raise the intriguing possibility that expanding loan programs have actually exerted a net deflationary impact on aggregate private demand. Whether the ex-penditure offsets to new loans have been that potent in the past is, for reasons given above, the moot question. There is very little doubt, however, that the active program of loan sales, inaugurated by the Kennedy administration and expanded by the Johnson administration, has permitted federal expenditures that otherwise would not have been made and have thereby contributed to the business expansion now nearing a record duration.

4

Basic Behavioral Patterns

FEDERAL LOAN PROGRAMS exhibit an almost bewildering variety of idiosyncrasies. Only a few of these features are of interest to anyone wishing to assess the potential contributions of federal lending to full employment and general price stability, and on these the present chapter will concentrate. Perhaps the most important of all for short-run flexibility are (1) the length and variability of the different stages through which loans and their economic effects must pass, and (2) the manner in which credit terms are set—whether by fixed or variable legislative formula or at the discretion of program administrators. In addition, the analysis of Chapter 2 stressed the need to segregate loans for marginal borrowers from those granted without such restrictions, to compare programs financed from the general fund with those having powers to sell their own debt to private investors, and to pay close attention to the mutual interactions between federal lending and other monetary and fiscal developments.

These, and other, basic behavioral patterns constitute the subject matter of the present chapter. In the first section, those lending programs are discussed whose characteristics qualify them as flexible, short-run stabilizers, using small business loans to illustrate the problems and potentialities involved. Other programs of this kind are treated briefly at the end of the section, and additional details are given in Appendix A. The second section also deals with a flexible type of lending, that of the Secondary Market Fund of the Federal National Mortgage Association. But separate treatment is justified by the opportunity this agency provides for contrasting different methods of financing and of observing various impediments to countercyclical behavior. The third section then turns to programs with relatively long and variable time lags, making their operations subject to only a limited amount of short-run variation. The chapter closes with an analysis of two new programs, national defense educational and area redevelopment loans, that offer considerable promise of alleviating chronic structural unemployment and hence of accelerating the rate of economic growth.

Flexible Stabilizers

To qualify as an effective moderator of economic fluctuations, a government loan program must satisfy two basic requirements. The first is that only a short period of time should elapse between the authorization of a loan, which is the control point of the program, and the occurrence of the resulting economic effects, and the second is that lending terms should not be so fixed that the program suffers from the perverse built-in cyclical sensitivity noted in Chapter 2. These qualities alone do not, of course, guarantee success in the stabilization field. Credit terms may be changed at the wrong times, and as will be shown below, the special needs of government borrowers will sometimes clash with the requirements of general economic policy.

Because they provide an excellent illustration both of the difficulties that are encountered and of the accomplishments that are possible, business loans of the Small Business Administration (SBA) have been selected for major attention in this section. At the end, however, the distinguishing features of other important stabilizers in the federal lending field are discussed briefly.

Federal Loans to Small Business

By far the largest of the Small Business Administration's four financial assistance programs,[1] business loans are also the most amenable to countercyclical variation. Unlike disaster loans, the need for them does not arise from unpredictable events occurring quite independently of business fluctuations; and unlike either the small business investment company or the state and local development company programs, SBA exercises close supervision over business loans and provides a major

[1] In mid-1963 business loans were 72 percent of SBA's total portfolio of $814 million, compared to 15 percent for small business investment company loans and debentures, 10 percent for disaster loans, and 3 percent for development company loans. For further details see App. A, MB-3, MB-7, and U-8.

share of the funds involved. Business loan applications can normally be processed in two months or less, and a similar interval typically elapses between the authorization and the disbursement of funds. Program liberalization as soon as the onset of a recession is recognized, therefore, could provide support to the economy before the end of even a short recession, and SBA has considerable administrative authority to initiate such policies on its own. The one major difficulty arises from the fact that the credit tightening needed to combat inflationary pressures conflicts with some of the goals regarded as appropriate for the federal government in the business area. If, as has frequently been argued,[2] small business suffers from a serious competitive disadvantage in obtaining medium- and long-term loans and equity capital, some federal financial assistance is needed, regardless of the state of the economy, until suitable private institutions fill in this particular credit gap. Moreover, it has also been argued that small businesses typically face increasing financial discrimination as monetary conditions tighten, and that SBA lending, therefore, should increase procyclically during a boom in order to moderate these inequities of general monetary policy.[3] The best example of these conflicts between stabilization and equity is provided by the 1955-57 boom, to be discussed in the next section.

To restrict its loans to marginal and submarginal borrowers SBA has established a detailed set of rules and procedures so that the applicant for a direct SBA loan encounters many tribulations. First, he must present convincing evidence of his inability to obtain sufficient funds from private lenders on reasonable terms; second, he must propose to the private lender, and have rejected by him, an SBA deferred participation loan agreement, under which the private lender would advance all of the loan funds, but SBA would be committed, on request,

[2] See, for example, "Small Business Financing: Corporate Manufacturers," *Federal Reserve Bulletin* (January 1961), pp. 8-22, and John McCroskey, "Federal Credit Programs for Small Business," in *Federal Credit Agencies*, a series of research studies prepared for the Commission on Money and Credit (Prentice-Hall, Inc., 1963), pp. 463-88.

[3] *Ibid.* This point of view was given official recognition in the *Economic Report of the President*, transmitted to the Congress January 1957, p. 42, and *ibid.*, January 1958, p. 7 (Government Printing Office, 1957 and 1958). For some opposing evidence, however, see G. L. Bach and C. J. Huizenga, "The Differential Effects of Tight Money," *American Economic Review*, Vol. 51 (March 1961), pp. 52-80.

to purchase up to 90 percent of the outstanding loan principal;[4] and last, he must find the private lender unwilling to make a loan jointly with SBA under an immediate participation agreement.

Some measure of the difficulties presented by the last two barriers is given by the fact that of all business loans approved by SBA through calendar 1962, slightly over 15 percent were deferred participations, 48 percent were immediate participations, and 37 percent were direct loans disbursed entirely by SBA.[5] In mid-1963, it was estimated that the total amount of business loans outstanding was $762 million, of which 77 percent was owed to SBA (on both direct and immediate participation loans and on any deferred participation portions purchased from the original lender), 7 percent constituted SBA's commitment to purchase deferred participation loans owed to private lenders, and the remaining 16 percent was held by private lenders entirely at their own risk.[6] Finally, a glance at the detailed listing of business loans approved, included as an appendix in SBA's regular reports, will indicate that the availability of government money at 5½ percent in recent years has not prevented the granting of many participation loans with rates ranging from 6 percent to 8 percent on the private lender's share.[7]

Several alternative quantitative measures of the initial impact of the SBA business loan program can be constructed. On the generous side would be a series that included not only SBA's direct loans and its commitments to purchase deferred participation loans but also the private lenders' shares of all immediate and deferred participation agreements. Although by no means a maximum estimate,[8] such a measurement would imply that all business loans, whether made at government or at private risk, represent a net addition to the flow of

[4] After July 1, 1963, SBA no longer agreed to purchase its share of a guaranteed loan on the request of the private lender but only on default by the borrower.

[5] Small Business Administration, *1962 Annual Report to the President and Congress*, p. 16.

[6] Computed from data given in *The Budget of the United States Government for the Fiscal Year Ending June 30, 1965, Appendix* (Government Printing Office, 1964), pp. 860-61.

[7] See, for example, pp. 98-159 of Small Business Administration, *1962 Annual Report*.

[8] One could also include whatever funds of their own SBA borrowers contribute to their loan-financed projects.

funds into the hands of small businesses. In all probability, such an assumption over-estimates the impact of the SBA, but increasingly conservative measures can be derived by subtracting from the gross loan series any or all of the following: (1) private lender shares of immediate participation loans, (2) private lender shares of deferred participation loans, (3) SBA commitments to purchase deferred participation loans, and (4) SBA loan disbursements used to refinance existing indebtedness. To exclude only the first item would be to argue that SBA guarantees typically stimulate the entire disbursement on a deferred participation loan and not just SBA's share of the transaction. On the other hand, elimination of the first three items would result in series showing only loans made with federal funds, implying therefore that SBA guarantees have no stimulating effects. Finally, since the expansionary powers of refinancing loans are ambiguous,[9] this type of SBA credit, which in recent years has varied between 29 percent and 37 percent of business loan approvals, might be segregated or even excluded entirely.[10] The effect of these adjustments in mid-1963 may be summarized as follows:

Gross business loans outstanding	$762 million
SBA share of loans outstanding	$636 million (items 1 and 2 subtracted)
SBA cash investment in loans outstanding	$585 million (items 1, 2, and 3 subtracted)
Estimated cash investment in non-refinancing loans outstanding	$400 million (all four items subtracted)

These figures give widely different measures of the initial economic impact of SBA business loans, but their movements over time have been sufficiently similar to permit the following discussion to be concentrated on the first and third.

Business Loan Reactions to Tight Money in 1955-1957

During the first half of 1955, Federal Reserve policy shifted steadily in the direction of monetary restraint, a condition that was then maintained until the third quarter of 1957. Under these and other pressures,

[9] See the discussion above in Chap. 2, p. 15.
[10] Small Business Administration, *4th Semiannual Report for Six Months Ending June 30, 1955* through *17th Semiannual Report, July 1-December 31, 1961.*

interest rates rose steadily from mid-1954 to late 1957, the increase accelerating after 1955. SBA during these years maintained its terms of credit relatively constant, and as would be expected under these conditions, the demand for its loans expanded greatly. The number of business loan applications received, for example, rose from a seasonally adjusted low of 220 a month in mid-1955 to a peak of 750 a month in late 1956 and then receded to a level of 500 a month by mid-1957 (Table A-2). Both approvals of, and net disbursements on, business loans rose more slowly and did not reach their peaks until the first half of 1957 (Table 4-1). In each case, however, the rise was substantial, approvals more than tripling and net disbursements quintupling, between the first halves of 1955 and 1957.

This expansion might well have been greater had not the business loan program faced a number of impediments during this period. SBA was first created only on a temporary basis, and its operations were slowed during the summer of 1955, when its lending authority expired at the end of June, and was not renewed until the second week of August. Then the occurrence of widespread natural disasters during the fall of that year diverted manpower to the disaster loan program, thus delaying the processing of business applications. Shortages of funds stopped the approval of business loans during the spring of 1956 and again for nearly three months in early 1957. At the same time, however, the agency, as it gained experience, steadily simplified and speeded up its administrative procedures, and the scope of its activities was gradually expanded to cover additional types of business enterprise.[11] Finally, the legislative amendments of 1955 increased size limitations on business loans and permitted SBA to charge interest rates below 6 percent in areas where such levels prevailed among private lenders.[12]

The 1955-57 expansion in SBA business loans, then, cannot be viewed solely as an automatic reaction by a fixed program to increasing monetary stringency. Numerous other factors were at work, but their effects were to some extent offsetting, and the automatic response

[11] See Small Business Administration, *4th Semiannual Report for Six Months Ending June 30, 1955* through *9th Semiannual Report for Six Months Ending December 31, 1957.*

[12] 69 Stat. 547, approved Aug. 9, 1955.

TABLE 4-1. *Small Business Administration Business Loan Approvals and Net Disbursements, Semiannually, 1953-1963*

(Millions of dollars)

Half-Year Period	Amount of Business Loans Approved, Seasonally Adjusted at Annual Rates (1)	Change in SBA's Cash Investment in Business Loans Out-standing, Annual Rates (2)	Change in the Gross Amount of Business Loans Out-standing, Annual Rates (3)
1953-II	$ 21	—	—
1954-I	57	$ 2	$ 10
-II	59	20	56
1955-I	45	13	15
-II	67	15	27
1956-I	95	33	49
-II	154	57	77
1957-I	163	74	94
-II	161	69	83
1958-I	223	83	104
-II	263	96	119
1959-I	270	116	146
-II	153	55	67
1960-I	181	48	45
-II	212	55	55
1961-I	283	57	76
-II	473	114	120
1962-I	267	168	237
-II	374	64	} 72
1963-I	264	28	

Sources: Small Business Administration, *Semiannual* and *Annual Report*, various years; *The Budget of the United States Government*, various years.

mechanism may consequently have played the leading role. In any case, SBA lending did expand procyclically at this time, giving rise to the controversy, already noted, over whether such behavior was defensible on equity grounds as an offset to the uneven impact of general monetary policies.

Business Loan Reactions to Two Recessions

By the business-cycle peak of July 1957 the Small Business Administration was a well-established lending agency, and it is interesting to compare the program developments that appear to have been affected by the 1957-58 recession with a similar set for 1960-61. In general, legislative changes were more important in the former period and administrative actions in the latter, lending terms were liberalized in both, and the business loan program contributed in each case to the expansion of aggregate demand needed to counteract excessive unemployment.

1957-1958. As was true throughout the federal government, SBA's reactions to the 1957-58 economic contraction were slow in coming, but administrative procedures were speeded up in various ways during the first half of 1958.[13] On the first of April, the month in which the recession ended, the fees charged on deferred participation agreements were cut in half, an action that helped to reverse, temporarily, an extended decline in the importance of this type of SBA loan.[14]

The most significant development in 1958, however, was the passage during the summer of the Small Business and Small Business Investment Acts, the former making SBA a permanent agency and liberalizing its lending terms, and the latter establishing a new credit program of great promise.[15]

The first important result of these actions was the reduction in the interest rate on business loans from 6 percent to $5\frac{1}{2}$ percent in July,

[13] Small Business Administration, *10th Semiannual Report for Six Months Ending June 30, 1958*, p. 32.

[14] From 50 percent of the total number of business loans approved through mid-1955, deferred participations declined to a low of 15 percent in the first half of 1958, recovered to nearly 17 percent in fiscal 1959 after the reduction in SBA fees, but then resumed their decline to 8 percent in 1960 and 1961.

[15] The laws were 72 Stat. 384, approved July 18, 1958, and 72 Stat. 689, approved Aug. 21, 1958. The small business investment company program is discussed in App. A, MB-7.

less than a month before the Federal Reserve returned to a policy of monetary restraint. It is difficult to tell whether this joint improvement in the attractiveness of SBA loans did much more than prolong an expansion that was already under way. The seasonally adjusted series for business loan applications began rising in the summer of 1957, reached a peak of just over 1,000 a month in May 1958, and then maintained this high level, in a rather erratic fashion, until early 1959 (Table A-2). The rapid rise in the spring of 1958, however, may have been largely attributable to uncertainties concerning the extension of SBA's existence beyond mid-1958; and had it not occurred, the impact of the 1958 credit liberalization on new inquiries might have been greater than it appears to have been. Despite the higher inflow of applications, business loan approvals and net disbursements fell slightly during the early months of the recession, but recovered in early 1958 and continued to rise through the first half of 1959 (Table 4-1).

1960-1961. During the two years following the business-cycle peak of May 1960 the business loan program expanded to peak levels (Table 4-1). Among the administrative actions contributing to these developments were processing speed-ups, additions to the list of eligible borrowers during the second half of 1960, and a liberalizing of collateral requirements and loan ceiling amounts during the first half of 1961. As in the preceding recession, the interest rate was lowered, the drop in April 1961 being larger in amount (from 5½ percent to 4 percent), but restricted this time to small businesses in "substantial labor surplus" areas (extended later to redevelopment areas). In the midst of these expansionary actions, however, a few developments of the opposite kind were also occurring. Funds became short in August 1961, inducing Congress to vote an extra $20 million, but not without complaints that may have made an impression. In any case, budgetary pressures led SBA on December 1 to lower the maximum amount of ordinary business loans it would approve.[16] Even so, the agency continued to approach its aggregate legislative loan limit rapidly, and in March 1962 approvals were halted completely except for the most urgent cases. Four months later, Congress increased SBA lending powers

[16] The reduction was from $350,000 to $200,000 for SBA's share of any one business loan application, and it remained in effect until October 1962. Firms in defense industries were exempted from the restrictions.

by $466 million, but it was less generous with appropriations, providing only $40 million when the backlog of approved loans awaiting funds was $60 million. As it turned out, 1962 business loan operations fell below 1961 levels, but not enough to prevent the year from being the second highest in SBA's history.[17]

Other Flexible Lending Programs

In addition to small business loans, four other major federal lending programs have had sufficiently short time lags to qualify them as potential postwar economic stabilizers: the now almost completely liquidated Reconstruction Finance Corporation (RFC), the nondisaster loans of the Farmers Home Administration, the special assistance mortgage operations of the Federal National Mortgage Association (FNMA) (that agency's secondary market operations also qualify but merit separate discussion in the next section), and the direct housing loans of the Veterans Administration (VA). Additional details for these programs are given in Appendix A; here the important and distinguishing features of each are discussed.

THE LAST DAYS OF THE RFC. Founded by a Republican administration in January 1932, the Reconstruction Finance Corporation led a full, but not always happy, life under the Democrats, and was finally abolished by the Republicans in a series of steps that began in July 1953. Since few major lending programs have yet reached a comparable point in their careers, it is the immediately following period that is most significant for purposes of this discussion. Liquidation proper began on September 28, 1953, when RFC's authority to make loans expired. The agency then had a portfolio of nearly $800 million, composed of outstanding loans of $687 million, commitments to make future disbursements of $82 million, and a contingent liability of $26 million on deferred participation loans. Adhering closely to congressional directives, RFC officials embarked quickly on a vigorous liquidation campaign involving negotiated sales of loan paper, carefully planned refinancings, principal prepayments when the borrower's financial condition permitted them, and the sale of certificates of interest in a $73

[17] Only 11,200 applications were received, compared to 13,700 in 1961; and approvals were $316 million, compared to $369 million in 1961. SBA net disbursements, on the other hand, were greater in 1962 than in 1961 (Table 4-1).

million pool of RFC business loans too small to be individually attractive to private lenders.[18] In this way, the corporation's loan portfolio was reduced by $320 million in only nine months, all of them characterized by general economic recession. Nor were these deflationary actions offset to any important degree by the Small Business Administration, whose lending powers began when the RFC's ended. The first SBA loans were authorized in November 1953, and by mid-1954 only $5 million of them were outstanding.

This picture changed abruptly as the recession ended and the subsequent recovery movement got under way. During fiscal 1955, for example, outstanding RFC loans were reduced by only $62 million[19] while total SBA credit rose by $52 million. Nevertheless, by the time the unemployment rate in the country had fallen below 5 percent (in early 1955), the liquidation of RFC loans was 45 percent complete. The whole episode provides an intriguing picture of the federal government taking advantage of its own easy money policy to offset some of that policy's countercyclical effects.

THE FARMERS HOME ADMINISTRATION. Well-equipped for stabilization purposes both by its short program lags (less than three months elapsing between authorization and disbursement of most loans) and by the wide variety of restrictions (all of them subject to countercyclical variation) placed on its loans, the Farmers Home Administration (FHA) presents a somewhat enigmatic postwar record. In large part, this is because some observers will attach primary importance to absolute changes in the flow of federal funds, while others will wish to stress relative changes. To the former, any increase in the amount of loans outstanding during a recession would be stabilizing, but to the latter, an increase that was less than the rise occurring during the preceding boom would be procyclical. Table 4-2, based on the seasonally adjusted series for direct FHA loans outstanding given in Appendix Table A-3, shows how different the two interpretations can be.

[18] For further details see U. S. Secretary of the Treasury, *Final Report on the Reconstruction Finance Corporation* (Government Printing Office, 1959), pp. 169-84.

[19] This figure underestimates the decline slightly because in mid-1954, when RFC's independent life ended and its loans were transferred to other federal agencies, $64 million of mortgages was merged with those of the Federal National Mortgage Association and became indistinguishable thereafter.

TABLE 4-2. *Cyclical Classification of the Behavior of Direct Farmers Home Administration Loans Outstanding*

Cyclical Phase	Absolute Change in Amounts Outstanding	Change in Outstandings Relative to Preceding Phase
Postwar Contractions (C) and Recoveries (R)		
1949 C	D	S
1950 R	N	S
1953–54 C	S	S
1954–55 R	D	D
1957–58 C	S	D
1958–59 R	S	S
1960–61 C	N	S
1961–62 R	S	S
Postwar Expansions[a]		
1947–48	S	[b]
1955–57	D	D
1959–60	D	N

S = stabilizing D = destabilizing N = neutral
[a] Korean War period excluded.
[b] Not available.

Whereas absolute changes were procyclical nearly as often as they were the opposite, relative changes were more frequently countercyclical. The difference between the two tests is well illustrated by the first postwar recession and recovery. Outstanding FHA loans did fall slightly in 1949 and then remained stable in the first half of 1950, but these changes were countercyclical when viewed against the considerably larger declines that had been occurring during the preceding business-cycle expansion.

FHA program changes, made frequently during the postwar period, were also mainly of a stabilizing nature. Of four increases in interest rates, three were made appropriately during economic expansions; of nine major program liberalizations, dealing either with maximum loan amounts and minimum down payments or with borrower qualifications and restrictions on the use of loan funds, six occurred during recessions or early economic recovery; and of five new types of loans made available, only one was authorized during expansion (Appendix A, MB-4e).

Particularly notable among the countercyclical changes were the two relaxations in eligibility requirements for farm housing loans adopted in 1958 and 1960 as deliberate antirecession measures, and among the less frequent procyclical policies were two that offer parallels with the record of the RFC and SBA described above. The farm housing program was allowed to expire in 1954 in spite of high unemployment and reinstated in 1956 in spite of threatening inflation. The procyclical expansion of all direct FHA loans between mid-1955 and mid-1957 was largely induced by the failure of farmers to participate fully in the economic boom of the period.

ONE BILLION FOR LOW- AND MODERATE-PRICED HOUSING MORTGAGES. In its special assistance functions, authorized in mid-1954, the Federal National Mortgage Association acquired one of the few federal loan programs with explicit, though limited, stabilization powers. These may be exercised, through the purchase of home mortgages, only when the President determines that a decline in home building is materially threatening the stability of a high-level national economy, and then only if there is enough unused spending authority already on the books or if Congress is persuaded to provide additional funds. To date, these emergency powers have not been invoked. In addition, however, the Special Assistance Fund has authority, some of it usable by the President at his discretion, to buy mortgages which, for one reason or another, are relatively unattractive to private investors, and during the 1957-59 recession and recovery, these powers were used in an important way.

One of the first moves of the Eisenhower Administration against the recession that began in July 1957 was the release by the President on March 7, 1958, of $200 million for the purchase by the Fund of low-cost housing mortgages ($10,000 or less). Less than a month later this new program was superseded by a much bigger one and ended its brief life with less than $2 million of mortgages purchased. The much bigger program was the $1 billion low- and moderate-priced housing mortgage ($13,500 or less) program authorized by Congress on April 1 and put into effect three days later.[20] At the same time, the President released $300 million under his own authority, which had been increased from $450 to $950 million by the same Housing Act. Clearly, the stage was set for important developments.

The new low- and moderate-priced mortgage program got under way very quickly. By the end of June, commitments of $412 million had been made, and by October 8 the entire $1 billion authority was exhausted. Apparently, builders did some stockpiling of these commitments, so that the primary economic effects of the program did not all begin before October 8.[21] Most of the effects, however, presumably occurred before FNMA's purchases of the mortgages involved. The tabulation below shows that nearly 80 percent ($657 million) of these had been made by mid-1959, at which time the economy had just passed from recovery to expansion.

Semiannual Period	Amount of Low- and Moderate-Priced Housing Mortgages Purchased (Millions)
1958-I	$ 0
-II	102
1959-I	555
-II	184
1960-I	2
Total	$843

The program consequently must have exerted most of its impact when the rate of unemployment in the country was relatively high. While in amount the impact certainly fell short of its full potential—nearly 20 percent of the original volume of commitments did not materialize in the form of purchases, and some of the purchases undoubtedly financed new housing that would have been constructed anyway—it seems clear that the total effect was an important one. Had the program been authorized as soon as the recession was generally recognized,

[20] 72 Stat. 73, approved April 1, 1958.
[21] Wilfred Lewis, Jr., *Federal Fiscal Policy in the Postwar Recessions* (Brookings Institution, 1962), p. 229.

say in late November 1957,[22] even more of its influence would have been felt before the end of the recovery period.

As far as fiscal offsets to the purchase of low- and moderate-priced mortgages are concerned, the discussion in Chapter 3 indicated that these would probably have taken the form of reduced expenditures for other purposes. Indeed, the effects in question might well have been felt within the Federal National Mortgage Association itself, high mortgage purchases by its Special Assistance Fund making possible greater mortgage sales by its Secondary Market Operations Trust Fund.[23] If this did occur, however, the resulting deflationary impact on mortgage markets, and on residential building generally, would come from FNMA secondary market policies and should not be regarded as a limitation to the expansionary power of the low- and moderate-priced mortgage program.

Quite apart from that program, FNMA's other special assistance functions were by no means languishing. New commitments in recession-dominated fiscal 1958 were at a peak level of $537 million, compared to $343 million in 1957 and $288 million in 1959. Mortgage purchases climbed rapidly throughout the recession and recovery, from only $24 million in fiscal 1957 to $145 million in 1958 and $409 million in 1959. Since then, in spite of a second major liberalization of the program made early in the recovery from the 1960-61 recession,[24] special assistance operations have expanded much less, the Fund's portfolio increasing by only $400 million during the next four years.

DIRECT HOUSING LOANS FOR VETERANS. The most distinctive features of the direct loan program of the Veterans Administration, set up in mid-1950 because of the scarcity of home loans guaranteed by the VA in the less populous parts of the country, have been its precarious existence (its life was extended by Congress nine times in the first eleven years) and the extent to which shortages of funds have curtailed its operations. Both characteristics are to a large extent attributable to a

---

[22] Based on a recent estimate by Rendigs Fels that "a consensus of informed observers" had recognized the July downturn by mid-November 1957. See his "The Recognition-Lag and Semi-Automatic Stabilizers," *Review of Economics and Statistics*, Vol. 45 (August 1963), p. 281.

[23] Lewis, *op. cit.*, p. 230.

[24] In the Housing Act of 1961, 75 Stat. 149, approved June 30, 1961.

lack of agreement about basic goals. Some think the interest rate on VA-guaranteed loans should be set sufficiently high to attract a plentiful supply of private funds, leaving direct VA loans to fill in a limited number of frictional gaps in private mortgage markets; others believe that the maximum interest rate on guaranteed loans should be set relatively low and that direct loans should be granted to all veterans unable to obtain private mortgages at that rate. Controversy over which of these alternatives, or what intermediate compromise, should be adopted has marked most of the career of the VA direct loan program and has added an erratic element to its postwar performance.

One cannot, therefore, infer its countercyclical powers from the record alone. Time lags are short, two months or less being required between the receipt of an application and the final closing of the loan agreement, and the program can consequently react quickly to business fluctuations. Perhaps the best example occurred during the 1957 recession when, because of the availability of funds withheld during the preceding boom and a favorable housing market, VA direct loans expanded rapidly. Other behavioral patterns, though not equally stabilizing, are similar to those exhibited by other lending agencies. The program, for example, has been sensitive to conditions in the industry it serves, as in fiscal 1960 when it reached its peak level of lending during an extended decline in residential construction. It has reacted to the state of the federal budget, as in 1962-63 when it embarked on an extensive loan sales campaign at least partly because of a rising federal deficit and an increasingly restrictive public debt ceiling. Also, it has been affected by the general state of the economy, as in 1958 and 1961 when major legislative liberalizations were made in its operations at, or shortly after, the end of general economic recessions.

Secondary Mortgage Market Operations
With Treasury and With Private Funds

The postwar record of the Federal National Mortgage Association is divided into two segments by the FNMA Charter Act of 1954.[25] Prior to that act, mortgage operations were financed entirely by the Treas-

[25] 68 Stat. 613, approved Aug. 2, 1954 to take effect Nov. 1, 1954.

ury, which at the end of 1954 had $2.4 billion invested in FHA and VA home mortgages and was committed to purchase an additional $0.5 billion. Thereafter, this original loan portfolio was segregated in a Management and Liquidation Fund, which by mid-1963 had reduced its mortgage holdings to less than $1.3 billion;[26] and active FNMA lending activities were divided between a Treasury-financed Special Assistance Functions Fund, already discussed above, and a Secondary Market Operations Trust Fund, which has drawn most of its money from private investors. It is this last program that is the chief concern here, but its accomplishments and potentialities can be brought out most clearly by comparing them with those of the pre-1954 program.

The most obvious difference between the two programs is the sharply reduced dependence of the current one on federal financing. Since 1954, the Treasury has invested $159 million in the preferred stock of the Secondary Market Trust Fund.[27] By mid-1963, it had received in return $138 million in the form of interest earnings, preferred stock dividends, and income taxes. What loans the Treasury has made to the Fund have all been short-term, and none were outstanding in mid-1963 when the Fund's indebtedness to private investors of $2.0 billion almost matched its total mortgage holdings of $2.1 billion. For all practical purposes, therefore, the Fund may be treated as a federally managed financial intermediary, borrowing from one private group in order to lend to another. Nevertheless, the Fund's authority to borrow up to $2.25 billion from the Treasury has certainly not been without influence. Because of it, the Fund has been freer to obtain its money by selling short-term discount notes, rather than long-term debentures, and all of its obligations may have been rendered less risky in the eyes of their purchasers, and hence salable at lower interest rates. A completely private secondary mortgage market institution would lack both of these advantages.

[26] This figure underestimates slightly the extent to which the original FNMA portfolio has been liquidated because the Management and Liquidation Fund has acquired a small number of mortgages from other federal agencies. In mid-1963, for example, it held $108 million in mortgages that it had purchased from the Public Housing Administration.

[27] $93 million of this was the Treasury's net worth in FNMA at Nov. 1, 1954, when lending authority under the original program expired.

Stabilization Problems and Potentialities

FNMA's Secondary Market Trust Fund differs from the loan programs discussed earlier in this chapter in three main ways: (1) FNMA lends to other lenders rather than to ultimate borrowers, and apart from its limited use of standby commitments,[28] it does not participate directly in the origination of new mortgages; (2) as just shown, FNMA mortgage purchases are financed mainly by the sale of securities to private investors rather than by the variety of sources available to a regular federal loan program; and (3) the agency services an industry which, as is well known, has behaved in a countercyclical way during the postwar period. Interestingly enough, each of these differences, and particularly the second, tends to complicate the task of using secondary mortgage market operations for stabilization purposes. The problems that emerge in each case are considered briefly below.

The fact that FNMA does not lend to home buyers but makes its purchases from mortgage companies, banks, and other financial institutions places an extra link in the chain by which the effects of its operations are transmitted to productive activity. Whereas a government loan to a submarginal borrower is a direct addition to the funds of an active spender on new output, a FNMA purchase of an existing mortgage simply enables the seller to supply additional loan funds to private borrowers, who may or may not wish to take them on the terms offered. The difficulty with the longer chain, specifically, is both that there is increased opportunity for the expansionary impact to be dissipated before it reaches new production and that, even if it is not dissipated, the whole process may take a relatively long time. Too little is known about either of these aspects of FNMA operations. The postwar behavior of residential construction, however, does suggest that the time lags are not excessively long, and as far as the size of the total impact is concerned, it may be noted that most FNMA credit has been extended on new houses. This does not mean, of course, that

[28] Between August 1956, when it first acquired the necessary authority, and mid-1963, the Secondary Market Fund has issued advance commitments of only $478 million, compared to total mortgage purchases of over $4.5 billion during the same period.

none of these new houses would otherwise have been built; but since residential construction is highly sensitive to credit market conditions,[29] the potential expansionary impact of FNMA operations may be close to the volume of purchases made.[30]

The main impediment to the realization of this potential is the deflationary influence that the sale of FNMA debentures may have on residential construction. Nothing would be accomplished, for example, if FNMA borrowed from a bank in order to lend to a home buyer when that home buyer could have sold his mortgage to the bank on exactly the same terms in the first place. If, on the other hand, FNMA differentiates its debt operations by issuing short-term, low-risk securities and using the proceeds to buy long-term, higher-risk mortgages, it may well bring about a significant shift of funds into residential construction. While to some extent the funds may be taken from other productive uses, the improvement made by the whole operation in both the liquidity and the quality of the financial assets available to private investors is likely to activate the existing money supply, so that home building does not increase entirely at the expense of other kinds of output.

In order to maximize its expansionary impact both on residential construction and on economic activity in general, then, the Secondary Market Fund should finance its mortgage purchases by borrowing short-term on the open market. As the economy moves back toward full employment, it could then place longer and longer terms on the securities it offers for sale, in order to offset more and more the demand-creating effects of its mortgage purchases. At the same time, however, it would increase its chances of taking funds from one group

[29] On this point see George F. Break, *The Economic Impact of Federal Loan Insurance* (National Planning Association, 1961), App. A; Leo Grebler and Sherman J. Maisel, "Determinants of Residential Construction: A Review of Present Knowledge," in Commission on Money and Credit, *Impacts of Monetary Policy* (Prentice-Hall, 1963); Tong Hun Lee, "The Stock Demand Elasticities of Non-Farm Housing," *Review of Economics and Statistics*, Vol. 46 (February 1964), pp. 82-89; and Richard F. Muth, "The Demand for Non-Farm Housing," in Arnold C. Harberger, ed., *The Demand for Durable Goods* (University of Chicago Press, 1960).

[30] Jack M. Guttentag, for example, takes this position in his study, "The Federal National Mortgage Association" in Commission on Money and Credit, *Federal Credit Agencies* (Prentice-Hall, 1963), pp. 103-07.

of home builders in order to give them to another. This kind of government loan program, in other words, is not an efficient method of bringing about a noninflationary increase in residential construction when the economy is at full employment.[31]

It could, however, given the will, act so as to reduce the demand for housing under general inflationary conditions. To do this, it should shift to the net sale of mortgages from its portfolio, and whenever its own short-term notes come due, replace them with long-term bonds. An excess of mortgage sales over purchases would, of course, mean an inflow of funds to the agency, and traditionally these would be used to retire its own outstanding debt. If too many financial conservatives were not looking over its shoulder, however, the agency might add all excess funds to its cash balances and keep its indebtedness at a relatively high level. In this way, it would maximize its tightening impact on private financial markets. Moreover, it would put itself in a position, when the next need arose to stimulate residential construction, to buy mortgages with its own funds and with no risk of discouraging spending in any part of the economy.

Such would be the life of the Secondary Market Fund if it were run by a group of dedicated economic stabilizers. Their accomplishments, however, would not be without their price. To sell mortgages on a tight money market, one might have to offer them at a price lower than that paid to acquire them; and to hold bigger and bigger money balances, when interest rates are high and one's own indebtedness has to be refunded on increasingly costly terms, would exercise remarkable restraint, particularly since federal trust funds are normally expected to earn their own way.

My conclusion, then, is that while a federal financial intermediary, like the FNMA secondary market operations trust fund, can contribute to economic stabilization, its powers in this regard are subject to important limitations. A regular direct loan program, in contrast, is considerably more flexible. It can more readily bring about a change in the composition of full employment output by having its loans financed with appropriate kinds of taxes or by occasioning a reduction in other kinds of federal expenditures. It can also maximize its expansionary

[31] *Ibid.*, pp. 111-13.

impact on aggregate demand by having new money created on the spot to finance its loans rather than first having to build up its idle money balances to a sufficiently high level, as must a financial intermediary. Alternatively, a direct loan program could behave like a financial intermediary, borrowing in order to lend; but even in this regard it would possess some advantages. Since the Treasury's debt can ordinarily be marketed at a lower interest rate, other things equal, than can the unguaranteed securities of a federal trust fund, a debt-financed direct loan program would be under less pressure to keep its revenues high in order to show a profit, and it would therefore be a little freer to adopt price policies conducive to economic stabilization.

Important as the methods chosen to finance secondary market operations undoubtedly are, it is even more important, from the point of view of economic stabilization, that the mortgage purchases and sales themselves be concentrated in the appropriate phases of the business cycle. As later discussion will show, FNMA's record in this regard is hardly an impressive one, and the main reason, paradoxically, appears to be that residential construction has in fact been an important stabilizer during the postwar period. The result has been to present federal policy makers with a difficult choice of what they should stabilize. If, during an inflationary period, they had undertaken to reduce the demand for housing, they might well have found themselves increasing a decline in home building that was already under way; and if, during a recession, they had attempted to expand housing demand, they might have so accelerated a housing boom that home costs and prices would have risen substantially.

Whether residential construction should be destabilized in order to stabilize the economy, if that is the choice that must be made, depends primarily on the mobility of the relevant resources. Certainly, it would be embarrassing to speed a decline in home building during a boom period like 1955-57 if all that happened was an increase in the rate of unemployment. Resources, however, are far from being completely specialized to home building, and on release from that activity, most of them would find employment elsewhere, particularly, as was the case in 1955-57, if commercial and industrial construction were rising rapidly. Tighter home mortgage markets during those years would have moderated the 15 percent increase in nonresidential construction prices that in fact occurred.[32] Conversely, a more rapid expansion in residential construction when the general rate of unemployment was high would be helpful so long as some of the idle resources could be used to build homes (because, say, nonresidential building was falling, as it was during the recessions of 1948-49 and 1957-58). If business building itself were booming, however, there would be little scope for employment-generating policies in the construction industry.

The extent to which secondary market operations in home mortgages should be manipulated by the government for stabilization purposes, then, depends primarily on the nature of the cyclical interactions among different parts of the construction industry. Since these cannot be foreseen with perfect accuracy, federal lending policies in this area, as in most others, should not be laid down in advance but should vary with the specific circumstances prevailing at the time. With these considerations in mind, the postwar stabilization record of FNMA secondary market operations will now be discussed.

Stabilization Record With Treasury Funds

Because of FNMA's quiescence before mid-1948 and the special features of the Korean War period, only two episodes are of interest, both marked chiefly by economic recession and recovery. The first, extending from mid-1948 to mid-1950, shows how rapidly federal lending can increase when the government is willing to make advance commitments to purchase mortgages at above-market prices.[33] From less than $150 million during the second half of 1948, FNMA purchase commitments rose to $557 and $799 million in the first and second halves of 1949 respectively; and although purchases lagged well behind, the net flow of credit to the private sector reached its peak annual rate of more than $700 million during the second half of 1949 (Chart 4-1).

The extensive use of advance commitments, which in effect moved the agency from the secondary to the primary mortgage market, meant that most of the initial economic impact of its operations preceded the purchases of the mortgages involved. The induced expansion in housing demand was consequently concentrated in the 1949 recession,

[32] The GNP price deflator for "other" construction rose from 101.1 in the first quarter of 1955 to 116.5 in the third quarter of 1957 at the business cycle peak.

[33] Guttentag, *op. cit.*, pp. 69-70. The policy in question was to purchase VA mortgages at par when they were selling at a discount on secondary markets.

CHART 4-1. *Federal National Mortgage Association Operations: Changes in Amounts of Loans Outstanding*

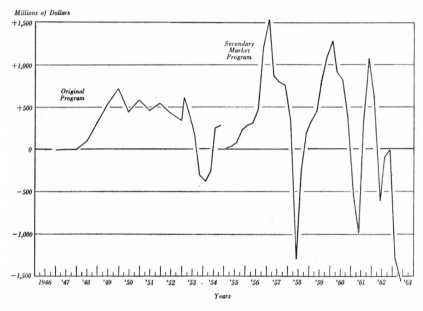

Millions of Dollars

Years

when residential construction was rising rapidly. Nonfarm housing prices, which had been rising throughout the 1946-48 postwar boom, fell off by about 7 percent during the first three quarters of 1949 and then rose by 11 percent over the next year. FNMA's contribution to the first part of the 1949-50 housing boom, therefore, was probably helpful both to the industry itself and to the economy as a whole. Later, however, the impact was at least partially dissipated in price increases.

As for fiscal offsets to FNMA mortgage purchases at this time, the discussion in Chapter 3 indicated that either higher taxes or increased debt sales were unlikely. Had the program expanded less rapidly during 1948-50, therefore, the economy might have had more government output but less residential construction in the first part of the period, whereas in the second part, it might well have had both more government services and lower housing prices.

On the face of it, FNMA's behavior during the second episode (the 1953-55 recession and recovery) was strongly procyclical. Mortgage sales rose from negligible amounts in early 1953 to over $200 million in the first quarter of 1954, and during the same period net disbursements sharply reversed themselves, from an annual outflow of $600 million to an inflow of nearly $400 million. During the rest of 1954, purchases once again exceeded sales, but the flow of funds into private hands remained well below 1950-52 levels. These figures cannot, however, be interpreted in the usual way, for FNMA activities at the time were dominated by a novel arrangement, known as the "one-for-one" program, adopted in response to the increasing unwillingness of private lenders in 1953 to commit themselves in advance to purchase federally underwritten home mortgages. This fiscal offset to tight monetary policy took the form of FNMA mortgage sales combined, in return for a small fee, with an agreement by the association to purchase from the buyer, any time within the following year, eligible mortgages up to the amount of the buyer's own purchases from FNMA. There was to be, in other words, no increase in FNMA's mortgage portfolio, but the disappearance of forward commitments by private lenders was matched by the appearance of government ones.

In the special circumstances of the time, the program apparently worked fairly well,[34] and its main expansionary effect must have occurred sometime between the late 1953 upsurge in FNMA mortgage sales and the subsequent purchases of "one-for-one" mortgages in 1954 and 1955.[35] Residential construction did turn up in late 1953, and Grebler has concluded that FNMA helped in bringing about that change, although it did not, in his view, make an important contribution to the succeeding housing expansion.[36] The episode provides an interesting illustration not only of monetary-fiscal interactions but also of the accomplishments that are sometimes possible within the confines of a balanced budget.

[34] *Ibid.*, pp. 143-45.

[35] Purchases under the program were $17 million in 1953, $229 million in 1954, and $188 million in 1955.

[36] Leo Grebler, *Housing Issues in Economic Stabilization Policy*, Occasional Paper 72 (National Bureau of Economic Research, 1960), p. 30.

Stabilization Record with Private Funds

When its secondary market operations trust fund was established in 1954, FNMA was directed by Congress to shift from its previous policy of buying mortgages at par to one of making purchases at market prices and to confine its operations to mortgages of the same general quality as those bought by private financial institutions. Buying and selling prices and fees were to be set so as to permit its activities to be fully self-supporting and to prevent excessive use of its facilities. The Association was authorized to borrow up to $1 billion from the Treasury (this was increased to $2.25 billion in 1957) and up to ten times its net worth from private investors. To provide for a gradual shift to private ownership, sellers of mortgages to FNMA were required to purchase common stock in the secondary market fund equal to 3 percent of the amount of their sales.[37]

A glance at Chart 4-1 will indicate that since 1955 FNMA secondary market operations have been consistently and strongly procyclical. Two major behavior patterns stand out.

REACTIONS TO TIGHT MONEY MARKETS AND DECLINING RESIDENTIAL CONSTRUCTION. One of the important effects of anti-inflationary monetary policy during the 1955-57 boom was a sharp reduction in the supply of funds for the purchase of home mortgages, and FNMA actions in 1956 were part of a general governmental response to what many regarded as excessive pressure on the housing industry, then in the middle of a three-year decline in its activities.[38] Congressional passage of a new housing act in August 1956[39] set the stage for a rapid increase in FNMA mortgage purchases by reauthorizing FNMA to issue forward commitments and permitting it to reduce its common stock subscription requirements, which were quickly lowered from 3 percent to 1 percent. Shortly thereafter, in the first quarter of 1957, secondary market mortgage purchases reached their postwar quarterly peak (Chart 4-1). The necessary funds came primarily from the sale of short-term

[37] For further details on these changes see U. S. Housing and Home Finance Agency, *Eighth Annual Report, 1954* (Government Printing Office, 1955), pp. 403-16, 503-06.

[38] For a detailed account of the actions taken see Grebler, *op. cit.*, pp. 70-76.

[39] 70 Stat. 1113, approved Aug. 7, 1956.

FNMA debentures, mostly in 1957, so that a net outflow of money to the private sector of over $300 million in the second half of 1956 was almost exactly reversed during the following six months (Table 4-3).

Borrowing short-term in order to purchase mortgages in large quan-

TABLE 4-3. *Net Money Flows from the Federal National Mortgage Association Secondary Market Operations Trust Fund to the Private Sector, Semiannually, 1955-1963*

(Millions of dollars)

Semi-annual Period	Change in the Amount of Mortgages Held by FNMA	Change in the Amount of FNMA Debentures and Discount Notes Outstanding	Net Loan Flow to the Private Sector (1)–(2)	Change in the Amount of FNMA Common Stock Held by Private Investors	Net Money Flow to the Private Sector (3)–(4)
	(1)	(2)	(3)	(4)	(5)
1955-I	$ 9		$ 9		$ 9
-II	76		76	$ 2	74
1956-I	148	$100	48	4	44
-II	415	100	315	7	308
1957-I	599	850	−251	10	−261
-II	388	265	123	8	115
1958-I	−242	−150	− 92	5	− 97
-II	− 13	− 65	52	1	51
1959-I	193	190	3	4	− 1
-II	476	350	126	10	116
1960–I	551	644	− 93	13	−106
-II	302	238	64	8	56
1961-I	−381	−324	− 57	3	− 60
-II	350	254	96	4	92
1962-I	− 1	105	−106	7	−113
-II	− 25	−135	110	3	107
1963-I	−709	−462	−247	1	−248

Source: Federal National Mortgage Association, *Semiannual* and *Annual Report,* various years.

tities was, of course, the prescribed stabilization policy for a recession and not for a boom of the proportions of 1955-57. Had residential construction, because of different FNMA policies, declined more rapidly than in fact it did, construction costs might well have been prevented from rising at all.

Whether anything was learned from this experience is debatable. When tight money and declining housing construction were combined once more in 1959-60, FNMA secondary market purchases rose almost as quickly as before, reaching their peak in the first quarter of 1960. This time, it is true, a persistent high rate of unemployment provided a justification for expansionary fiscal policies, but construction prices nevertheless rose slowly between the end of the recovery in the second quarter of 1959 and the beginning of the recession a year later.[40] To complicate the picture still further, it may be noted in Table 4-4, FNMA concentrated its borrowings this time in the medium-term range of maturities, keeping the average unexpired term of its outstanding debentures at 3.25 years between mid-1959 and mid-1960. Apart from this difference in borrowing policy, fiscal 1960 operations were virtually identical with those of fiscal 1957 (Table 4-3), and one is tempted to conclude that, if anything, less expansionary impact was exerted in 1960 when it was more needed.

REACTIONS TO MONETARY EASE AND RISING RESIDENTIAL CONSTRUCTION. After purchasing episodes of the proportions just described, any mortgage lender, particularly one under instructions to avoid excessive use of his facilities, is likely to watch closely for the next profitable opportunity to dispose of some of his purchases. In neither instance did FNMA have long to wait, for within a few months the economy turned into recession, money markets were eased, and the prices of existing long-term securities turned upward. Taking advantage of these opportunities for profitable mortgage sales, the FNMA rapidly reduced both its mortgage holdings and its own indebtedness during the first halves of 1958 and 1961 (Table 4-3). While there was little net money flow between FNMA and the private sector in either of the fiscal years in which the recessions were concentrated (1958 and 1961), one important change occurred in the character of FNMA's outstanding de-

[40] The two GNP deflators for new construction (1954 = 100) rose from 114 to 116 (residential nonfarm) and from 120 to 122 (other).

TABLE 4-4. *Average Maturity of Federal National Mortgage Association Debentures Issued and Outstanding, 1956-1963*

Year and Quarter	Average Maturity of New Debentures Issued (years)	Average Unexpired Term of Debentures Outstanding at End of Period (years)
1956-1	0.75	
-2	—	0.67
-3	0.75	
-4	0.75	0.5
1957-1	0.8	
-2	0.9	0.6
-3	0.9	
-4	4.1	1.0
1958-1	4.5	
-2	—	2.8
-3	0.6	
-4	3.0	4.0
1959-1	1.0	
-2	3.1	3.25
-3	1.1	
-4	0.6	2.5
1960-1	4.8	
-2	3.1	3.25
-3	10.4	
-4	6.0	3.8
1961-1	—	
-2	8.4	5.25
-3	5.8	
-4	6.3	5.25
1962-1	15.0	
-2	—	6.17
-3	3.5	
-4	—	5.92
1963-1	—	
-2	—	5.92

Sources: Average Maturity computed, using the amounts of the different issues as weights, from data given in FNMA *Semiannual Reports*. Average unexpired term through Dec. 31, 1958 computed as above. Thereafter taken directly from FNMA *Semiannual Reports*.

bentures. Between mid-1957 and the end of 1958 the average unexpired term of these securities was raised from less than a year to four
years; and between mid-1960 and mid-1961 another increase, from $3\frac{1}{4}$
to $5\frac{1}{4}$ years, was brought about (Table 4-4).

Note once again the consistent pursuit of fiscal policies with destabilizing effects. With more mortgages and longer-term FNMA debentures in their hands, private investors could be expected to provide
less financial support for home building than they otherwise would
have. Since residential construction at the time was either stable or
rising, however, these effects were not readily observable, particularly
by those who believed that under conditions of monetary ease financial markets were capable of absorbing large quantities of new securities with no deflationary impact on private spending.

Although FNMA secondary market operations were broadly similar
in 1957-59 and 1960-61, a few differences are worth noting. Whereas
during the first recession and recovery there were three purchase price
reductions and only two increases, during the second period of high
unemployment there were seven purchase price increases and only one
reduction.[41] No change was made in the 2 percent common stock subscription requirement in 1957-59, but it was lowered to 1 percent between February and December 1961.[42] Finally, the Housing Act of
1961 authorized a new program (so far little used) under which
FNMA could make its own direct, short-term loans on the security of
federally underwritten mortgages.[43] All of these differences indicate a
more expansionary attitude on the part of the government in 1960-61.

[41] U. S. Housing and Home Finance Agency, *Eleventh Annual Report 1957* through
Fifteenth Annual Report 1961. In the former period, the price reductions came both
early and late (August and October 1957 and May 1959), while the countercyclical
price increases centered around the business-cycle trough (February and May 1958).
In the latter period, the price increases were bunched in the summer of 1960 (July
and August) and during the Kennedy Administration's big antirecession push from
February to May 1961.

[42] The return to 2 percent in late 1961 had both contractionary and expansionary
features. While the increase reduced the attractiveness of mortgage sales to FNMA,
the hope was that they would decline only moderately, so that FNMA's total capital
would increase, thus permitting increased sales of debentures, then restricted by the
ten-times net-worth requirement. Increased debenture sales, in turn, would permit
increased mortgage purchases by FNMA.

[43] See U. S. Housing and Home Finance Agency, *Fifteenth Annual Report, 1961*
(Government Printing Office, 1961), p. 245.

A close inspection of Chart 4-1 shows both a less severe decline and a more rapid rise in FNMA's portfolio during that period.

According to the dates in this study the recovery phase of the business cycle ended in the fourth quarter of 1961, but the succeeding expansion conspicuously lacked some of the important features of its immediate predecessors. Unemployment stayed high, money markets were relatively easy (although short-term interest rates did rise after mid-1963), and residential construction continued to rise, slowly at first but more rapidly in 1963. FNMA reacted consistently to these conditions, high sales and low purchases quickly shifting it to a net seller position that reached record proportions during the first half of 1963 (Chart 4-1).

Long-Lag Programs

Long and variable time lags, between the receipt of an application and the approval of the loan in question and between that approval and the occurrence of a significant volume of the loan's first-round economic effects, seriously impair a loan program's usefulness for short-run economic stabilization. They do not, however, completely eliminate it. Long processing lags can be offset by maintaining loan reviews at a high level during a period of credit restraint, building up a backlog of evaluated applications, and then releasing these as soon as a downturn in general business activity becomes clearly apparent. Slowly developing economic effects, it is true, are not controllable, except within narrow limits,[44] but loan approval early in a recession can still, in some cases, produce a significant expansionary impact before the end of the following recovery.

From the major federal loan programs with long or variable time lags (or both), five have been selected for study in this section. These are the college housing program, electric and telephone loans of the

[44] Individual projects within a program may involve widely varying time lags. Where there are enough short-lag undertakings available to make a difference, some advantage could be gained during periods of underemployment by giving them priority. The bottlenecks that typically slow down operations are also of varying seriousness, and these are minimized during periods of economic slack. At such times, therefore, projects can be carried out more rapidly than available measures of time lags indicate, since these are based on average situations.

Rural Electrification Administration, and development project and exporter loans of the Export-Import Bank of Washington. These accounted for over 25 percent of all direct federal loans outstanding in mid-1963. College housing loans and the two REA programs also provide an interesting contrast in interest rate policies, the former using a legislatively prescribed formula to vary the rate annually, and the latter maintaining throughout the postwar period a low 2 percent rate that for some years has been the object of much controversy.

College Housing Loans

From start to finish—that is, from the filing of a preliminary application with the Housing and Home Finance Agency to the completion of construction—it is not unusual for a college housing project to take over three years. The main stages into which that period may be broken, together with some estimates, based on loans approved in fiscal 1957, of the length of time taken for each, are given in Table 4-5.

In that year HHFA review of preliminary applications took 2½ months on the average, and if the decision was favorable, funds were

TABLE 4-5. *College Housing Program Stages and Average Time Lags for Loans Approved in Fiscal 1957*

(Months)

Program Stage	First Quartile	Median	Third Quartile	Arithmetic Mean
From filing of preliminary application to the reservation of funds	1	2	3	2½
From reservation of funds to loan approval	4	7	10	7
Total processing time	5	9	13	9½
Loan approval to start of construction	2	5	10	6½
Loan approval to sale of project bonds	8	13	19	14½
Loan approval to completion of construction	12	17	26	19½
Total time from start to finish	17	26	39	29

Source: Computed from data tabulations made available by the Finance Branch, Community Facilities Administration, Housing and Home Finance Agency. Quartiles and median computations were carried to the nearest month, and arithmetic means to the nearest half-month.

immediately set aside, or reserved, for the applicant, who then began filling out the detailed application required for final decision.[45] On the return of this full application to HHFA, a thorough and extensive analysis was made of the proposal, and final approval typically came seven months after funds had first been reserved for the project. All in all, then, government processing took a little over three-quarters of a year, but with a fairly wide range of variation around that average.

Approval of a college loan application commits HHFA to purchase the applicant's bonds if no equally good private offer is obtained at an open sale, and approval, therefore, is the final control point as far as the government is concerned. Unless processing time can be reduced, countercyclical variations in the program designed to alter the inflow of preliminary applications would not be an effective way of combating recessions as short as those since 1945. In a period of rising construction prices, however, the rate of final loan approvals could be slowed, or even stopped; and once a backlog of processed projects had been created, the program would be in a position to expand rapidly, should the level of construction begin to fall off.

Even then, however, the economic effects would not appear quickly. For college loans approved in fiscal 1957, construction did not begin, on the average, for $6\frac{1}{2}$ months and then lasted for another 13 months (Table 4-5). Perhaps half of the initial economic impact would occur within ten months of loan approval;[46] and within 15 months the project bonds would be offered for sale, HHFA disbursements would be made (in the absence of a competing private offer), and the project would be 80 percent finished. If allowance is made for a recognition lag of four months,[47] therefore, a relatively fast-developing project (at the first quartile) would have a significant impact before the end of most recessions, but the effects of other projects would be delayed until the recovery period or later.

[45] For additional details on these procedures see Arnold H. Diamond, "The College Housing Program: Its History and Operations," *The Educational Record* (July 1957).

[46] This estimate is based on the assumption that the value put in place each month on college housing construction is similar to that for private nonresidential building construction, for which a twelve-month total construction period has been given. See Thomas Mayer, "The Inflexibility of Monetary Policy," *The Review of Economics and Statistics,* Vol. 40 (November 1958), p. 362.

[47] Cf. Fels, *op. cit.,* p. 281.

TABLE 4-6. *Average Number of Days Required for Processing Rural Electrification Administration Loans, by Fiscal Year, 1956-1960*

Fiscal Year	Electric Loans		Telephone Loans	
	Regular	Short Form	New Borrowers	Established Borrowers
1956	154	63	359	152
1957	112	69	297	187
1958	101	71	281	173
1959	80	53	288	190
1960	85	43	257	268

Source: U. S. Department of Agriculture, Rural Electrification Administration.

The record provides one example of moderately successful anticyclical policy. Fund shortages held up loan approvals in 1960 until Congress voted an extra $500 million in September, four months after the business-cycle peak. As approvals quickly increased to more than double their earlier levels, President Eisenhower directed HHFA to give priority to projects on which construction could begin quickly. While the effects of these actions cannot be observed in isolation, it may be noted that quarterly increases in loans outstanding were unusually high after the first quarter of 1962 (Appendix B), indicating the occurrence of significant expansionary effects in late 1961 before the end of the recovery.

Since 1955, college housing interest rates have been based on the average rate on all interest-bearing federal debt,[48] but because changes are made only once a year, procyclical variations have not been avoided. At the beginning of the last two recessions, for example, increases of $\frac{1}{8}$ percent and $\frac{3}{8}$ percent, respectively, were made and then maintained throughout both periods of economic contraction. Long time lags, however, probably kept these actions from having the destabilizing impact they might have had for a more flexible program.

Rural Electric and Telephone Loans

Since the typical project supported by Rural Electrification Administration loans involves heavy construction of a complicated technical

[48] A $\frac{1}{4}$ percent allowance for administrative expenses is added, and the rate so determined cannot be less than $2\frac{3}{4}$ percent.

and economic nature, both the processing of loan applications and the disbursement of funds tend to proceed slowly. An electric loan application from an established borrower may be evaluated in a month; but proposals requiring a full feasibility study are likely to require three months or more, and the analysis of telephone loan projects has typically occupied the better part of a year (Table 4-6). After a loan has been approved, funds are normally advanced as the different phases of construction are completed. Table 4-7 shows that this stage of the program, during which the majority of the first-round economic effects are generated, is usually spread over several years, with considerable variation from one project to another.

The REA program, therefore, cannot readily be used for short-run economic stabilization. Even though the processing of applications may be speeded up in various ways, as it was during the 1953-55 recession and recovery, most of the expansionary effects are likely to be delayed by one to two years, or even more. Similar drawbacks apply

TABLE 4-7. *Percentages of Funds Advanced in Different Years After Loan Approval, for Electric Loans Made in Fiscal 1953-1957 and Telephone Loans Made in Fiscal 1956-1960*

(Percent)

Period	Electric Loans		Telephone Loans			
			New Borrowers		Established Borrowers	
	Average	Standard Deviation	Average	Standard Deviation	Average	Standard Deviation
Year in which loan is approved	8.2	3.0	9.7	3.5	7.2	2.4
First year following	28.5	4.0	30.1	6.6	40.8	4.7
Second year following	23.0	4.5	32.3	1.5	28.0	2.4
Third year following	16.0	4.6	14.6	1.4	17.3	9.0
Fourth year following	8.7		2.1		3.2	
Totals	84.4		88.8		96.5	

Source: U. S. Department of Agriculture, Rural Electrification Administration.

to the slowing down of loan approvals during a period of inflationary pressure.

Since the interest rate on them has been kept at 2 percent REA loans have increased markedly in attractiveness whenever private money markets have tightened, notably in 1956-57 when Moody's Aaa bond yields rose from 3 percent to nearly 4 percent and again in 1959-60 when Moody's yields reached nearly 4½ percent. During both periods, REA loan applications gave evidence of responding significantly to interest rate differentials. Seasonally adjusted electric applications, for example, rose from annual rates of $200 million in 1955 and the first half of 1956 to a rate well over $300 million during the next year and a half, and a similar increase occurred between 1958 and the first half of 1960 (Table A-6). The procyclical character of a fixed-interest-rate loan program is apparent, but in this case long time lags probably shifted most of the economic impact of these developments to the following recession and recovery periods, or even later. Electric loan net disbursements, for example, did not rise much until early 1957 and then stayed at high levels through early 1960 (Table B-9).

Export-Import Bank Loans

The domestic demand-creating effects of Eximbank loans are highly variable both in magnitude and in the speed with which they occur after the loan has been authorized. In recent years, the Bank has made four different kinds of direct loans:

1. Development project loans finance the acquisition of capital goods and equipment to be used in developing the economy of the borrowing country. Both the projects and the loans tend to be long-term and, as shown below, the loans are typically authorized months, or even years, before the items to be purchased with them are ready for export from this country.

2. Exporter loans are medium-term credits (one to five years) granted at the request of a United States exporter to help finance his sales abroad. In these cases, the foreign purchaser pays at least 12 percent of the total cost from his own funds, the exporter finances 20 percent himself, and Eximbank lends the remaining 68 percent to the foreign buyer. The total amount of the financed transaction, in other words, is at least 147 percent of Eximbank's loan, but this does not

mean, of course, that all of it is a net addition to the demand for United States goods.

3. Commodity loans are relatively short-term (up to fifteen months) and have been used mostly to finance the export of cotton, although other surplus agricultural products have also been involved. The principal economic effect of these loans has probably been to reduce the federal government's excess commodity inventories, with little or no impact on domestic output or employment.

4. Emergency foreign trade loans are granted to foreign countries with balance of payments difficulties that otherwise might cause them to restrict their imports from the United States. How much of a restriction would have occurred is always difficult to determine, and the expansionary effects of some of these loans may have been very small indeed. In June 1962, for example, Canada obtained a short-term standby credit of $400 million, but partly because of its success in obtaining long-term private loans and partly because of an improvement in its balance of payments, Canada was subsequently able to cancel all of the Eximbank credit without having used it. How much contribution this particular loan made to the maintenance of United States exports is clearly highly conjectural.

While precise measures of the expansionary powers of these four different types of loans cannot be derived, one simple procedure is to segregate development project and exporter credits on the argument that their impact on the demand for domestic output is significantly greater, on the average, than that of the other two types. The effects of doing this for the post-Korean period may be seen in Table 4-8. Although the two series shown tend to move in the same direction, the magnitudes of the implied economic effects diverge widely, particularly in fiscal 1954, 1958-59, and 1962.

In addition, development project and exporter loan disbursements, which are usually made when the goods being financed are ready for export, tend to lag, sometimes substantially, behind loan approvals, which typically set the first-round economic effects in motion. To estimate the length of these lags, a study was made of all development and exporter loans authorized from the second quarter of 1955 through the last quarter of 1956. Since the period selected forms the first part of the 1955-57 business-cycle expansion, interest centers on the propor-

TABLE 4-8. *Export-Import Bank Loan Disbursements by Major Type and Fiscal Year, 1954-1963*

(Millions of dollars)

Fiscal Year	Development Project and Exporter Loans	All Loans
1954	$111	$443
1955	109	154
1956	131	186
1957	169	230
1958	364	846
1959	456	709
1960	357	421
1961	461	526
1962	532	903
1963	461	508

Source: Table A-12.

tion of disbursements made before the beginning of the next recession. The results, which are given in Table 4-9, indicate clearly that both types of loan are subject to long and highly variable lags and hence cannot be classified as flexible stabilizers.[49]

Other Programs

Similar conclusions can be drawn for many of the foreign-aid loans of the Agency for International Development and its predecessors. Disbursement of development loans approved in 1959, for example, typically did not begin for nine and a half months and then was expected to be spread over the next three or four years.[50] Direct housing loans for the elderly also appear to be characterized by long time lags although the program was begun too recently (September 1959) to justify systematic analysis. It may be noted, however, that during its first year of effective operations (October 1960 through September 1961) preliminary loan approvals of $24 million were made, compared

[49] It may be noted that no countercyclical actions were taken during the 1953-54 and 1957-58 recessions and that what was done in 1961 applied mainly to the risk insurance program rather than to direct loans. See Export-Import Bank of Washington, *Report to the Congress for the Twelve Months Ending June 30, 1961*, pp. 15-16.

[50] U. S. House Appropriations Committee, *Mutual Security Appropriations for 1960*, p. 1055, and for *1961*, Part I, p. 348.

TABLE 4-9. *Export-Import Bank of Washington, Amount of Development Project and Exporter Loans Authorized in 1955 and 1956 and Percentages Disbursed by Mid-1957*

Year and Quarter	Amount of Loans Authorized in Quarter (Millions)	Percentage of Loans Disbursed by Mid-1957[a]
Development Project Loans		
1955-2	$16	75
1955-3	31	30
1955-4	24	5
1956-1	141	10
1956-2	69	4
1956-3	321	2
1956-4	11	45
Exporter Loans		
1955-2	22	45
1955-3	13	60
1955-4	17	15
1956-1	1	35
1956-2	2	40
1956-3	10	1
1956-4	32	20

Source: Computed from data given in Export-Import Bank of Washington, *Semiannual Report to the Congress,* various years.

[a] Percentages were computed from figures carried to the nearest tenth of a million, and those above 10 percent were rounded to the nearest 5 percent.

to only $5 million of final approvals and less than $500,000 of actual disbursements (Table A-7). Final approvals did not reach $24 million until the second quarter of 1962, and loans outstanding did not rise to the same level until shortly after mid-1963.

It is clear that long-lag programs, with their limited short-run flexibility, form an important part of federal lending operations. Nor does this exhaust the list of direct loans lying largely outside the scope of business-cycle policy making. Defense production loans, for example, are presumably based on the requirements of national security, rather than on the needs of economic stabilization, but with average annual gross disbursements of only $36 million (1951-63), the program has not been a major one. Much more interesting are two relatively new programs which, while capable of contributing to the alleviation of cyclical increases in unemployment, hold out still greater promise of reducing chronic structural unemployment and keeping it at levels low enough to permit realization of the economy's full growth potential. These programs are discussed in the next section.

Federal Lending and Structural Unemployment

There is no need to enter here into the current debate concerning how much of the excess unemployment in recent years is structural, rather than attributable to deficient aggregate demand. Suffice it to note that unemployment rates are chronically high among those with relatively little education, that future shifts in the importance of different industries and future technological developments are almost certain to raise average educational requirements, and that economic growth itself is likely to flounder unless the labor force is sufficiently well-educated to be receptive to the acquisition of new skills.[51] In such circumstances the potential contribution of federal educational loans, such as those authorized by Title II of the National Defense Education Act of 1958 (72 Stat. 1580), is very great indeed.[52]

National Defense Educational Loans

Student loans, which are advanced and administered by colleges and universities, are financed 90 percent by the federal government (in the form of annual contributions to Student Loan Funds) and 10 percent by the participating educational institutions. Not only are these loans low-rate (3 percent) and long-term (10 years), but neither repayment nor the accrual of interest begins until one year after the student has ceased to pursue a full-time course of academic study; and as much as 50 percent of the loan principal can be canceled for those going into public school teaching at the elementary or secondary level.[53] By mid-1962 loans of $220 million had been made, and $5 million, or more than twice the amount due, had been repaid.[54]

---

[51] For a discussion of these matters see the *Economic Report of the President*, transmitted to the Congress January 1964 (Government Printing Office, 1964), pp. 98-103, 110-11, and 172-83.

[52] The 1958 act authorized loans for educational institutions as well as for students, but the former have so far played a minor role (App. A, U-7).

[53] This is done at the rate of 10 percent of the loan principal plus accrued interest for each year of full-time public school teaching, subject to a maximum of 50 percent.

The economic significance of the student loan program depends very much on how many students who otherwise would not obtain a higher education are enabled by it to do so. While it is still too early to expect a definitive answer to this question, a sample survey of student borrowers during the summer and fall of 1960 indicated a high degree of success at that time. Over 91 percent of the students questioned indicated that national defense loans had made college educations possible for them, 25 percent being freshmen who were enabled to enter, 58 percent undergraduates who were enabled to continue, and 8 percent graduate students who otherwise would have had to give up, or at least postpone, full-time work toward higher degrees.[55] It is also interesting to note, in the same survey, that two out of every five student borrowers came from families with annual incomes of $4,000 or less, while five out of seven came from families whose incomes were $6,000 and under.[56] These figures are in sharp contrast to those for fellowships and scholarships, which go mainly to children from the middle and upper income groups.[57]

It is impossible at this point to make any quantitative projections of the future importance of federal loans for education at all levels, particularly since the national defense program itself is still on a temporary basis.[58] Nevertheless, there are a number of reasons for believing that currently authorized levels ($135 million in federal contributions plus $15 million in private matching funds for fiscal 1965) could be expanded materially.

In 1960 students participating in the national defense program indicated that they would be willing, on the average, to borrow $2,360 to finance their education, which is approximately $570 a year for a four-year college course.[59] If funds were available, therefore, the

---

[54] U. S. Department of Health, Education, and Welfare, *Report on the National Defense Education Act, Fiscal Years 1961 and 1962* (Government Printing Office, 1963), pp. 7 and 64.

[55] U. S. Department of Health, Education, and Welfare, *Student Borrowers: Their Needs and Resources* (Government Printing Office, 1962), p. 64. The report was written by Robert C. Hall and Stanton Craigie.

[56] *Ibid.*, p. 54.

[57] *New York Times* (July 28, 1963), p. 22.

[58] 77 Stat. 403, approved Dec. 18, 1963, extended the student loan program through fiscal 1965, authorizing $135 million for federal contributions in that year.

[59] *Student Borrowers: Their Needs and Resources, op. cit.*, p. 66. The average given in the text was computed by weighting the mid-points of the class intervals

314,000 students expected to participate during 1965 might well be willing to borrow $180 million.

In his 1962 Message on Education, President Kennedy indicated that among the members of the 1961 high school graduating class who did not enter college that fall were "200,000 who ranked in the upper 30 percent of their class, of whom one-third to one-half failed to go on to college principally because of a lack of finances."[60] The latter group alone would need loans of $40 million to $57 million at $570 per student per year, and as will be seen below, these amounts are likely to fall far short of their total financial requirements.

Tuition-free, public higher education is far from costless to the student. The major financial burden is his foregone earnings which currently must average at least $2,400 a year.[61] It is not to be expected that these sums, which would exceed $240 million a year for every 100,000 students educated, would, or even should, all be provided by federal loans. For many impoverished students, however, their availability in some form or other is probably a prerequisite for attendance at college or university.

The crucial question, then, is how sensitive will the demand for student loans be to changes in the terms on which they are offered. While ten-year, 3 percent, deferred-payment loans may be thought to be close to the ultimate in liberal credit terms, there are still good reasons for supposing that increased demands for loan funds could materialize in the future. Not only are social objections to borrowing to finance one's education disappearing—a trend in which the national defense education act itself has had no small part[62]—but economic re-

---

given on p. 66 by the percentage of students falling in each. For the top class of students willing to borrow over $6,000 (4.65 percent of the total group) $6,000 itself was used as a minimum measure.

[60] *Wall Street Journal* (Feb. 7, 1962).

[61] Theodore W. Schultz, in "Capital Formation by Education," *Journal of Political Economy*, Vol. 68 (December 1960), pp. 571-83, estimated the 1956 earnings foregone by college students to be $1,947, and this figure becomes $2,492 when it is adjusted for the 28 percent increase in the average gross earnings of manufacturing workers between 1956 and the last quarter of 1963. In addition, Schultz's estimate has been criticized as being too low by Rudolph C. Blitz, whose calculations would yield a current figure of $2,623. See U. S. Department of Health, Education, and Welfare, *Economics of Higher Education*, edited by Selma J. Mushkin (Government Printing Office, 1962), pp. 390-403.

[62] *Departments of Labor and Health, Education, and Welfare Appropriations for*

search is providing better and better estimates of the private profit to be realized from further education.[63] Properly publicized and understood, both of these developments should raise the demand for student loans at existing credit terms. In addition, these terms could be liberalized still further, say by lengthening maturities, by deferring repayments whenever the borrower's earning ability becomes temporarily impaired,[64] or, if a more imaginative arrangement is desired, by making repayments contingent on the borrower's receiving income above a stated minimum level.[65]

In addition to the expansion of lending under the national defense education program, other aspects of the structural unemployment problem could be brought under attack. Federal loans, for example, could be offered to offset earnings foregone when a high-school dropout returns to finish his education, when young people wish to acquire special technical abilities, or when adults have to replace obsolete accomplishments with new skills. While not specifically mentioned in President Johnson's Special Message on Poverty,[66] such loans could be a useful addition to the program there proposed.

Area Redevelopment Loans

Of all existing lending programs, the one most closely connected with structural unemployment is under the jurisdiction of the Area Redevelopment Administration, set up in the Department of Commerce in May 1961 (75 Stat. 47) to help communities suffering from either long-term unemployment or chronically low levels of family income. Like its older, and much bigger, cousin in the foreign aid area, the Area Redevelopment Administration program provides technical assistance at the planning level, helps workers acquire new skills, and makes both grants and loans to stimulate economic development.

The loans, which may be made either to state and local governments

---

1964, Hearings before the House Appropriations Committee (Government Printing Office, 1963), p. 498.

[63] See, for example, W. Lee Hansen, "Total and Private Rates of Return to Investment in Schooling," *Journal of Political Economy*, Vol. 71 (April 1963), pp. 128-40.

[64] Under present law loan repayments are canceled if the borrower dies or becomes totally and permanently disabled.

[65] As proposed by William Vickrey in "A Proposal for Student Loans," *Economics of Higher Education, op. cit.*, pp. 268-80.

[66] *New York Times*, March 17, 1964, p. 22.

or to nonprofit organizations representing redevelopment areas, carry relatively low rates of interest (3½ percent-4 percent) and long terms to maturity (25-40 years). They may be used to construct commercial, industrial, or public facilities; but obtaining them is not simply a matter of appearing on the scene with blueprints in hand. First the area in question must be officially designated as a redevelopment area (there were 933 such areas in the country at mid-1962),[67] and the project to be supported must be an integrated part of a general program for economic development. The project must be important enough to provide more than a temporary alleviation of unemployment; but if it involves the relocation of business enterprises, it must not cause unemployment in the area from which they came (the anti-piracy clause). A final restriction is that loans will be granted only if financial assistance is not available from private lenders or federal agencies on reasonable terms.

In part because of difficulties with the anti-piracy clause, operations did not become substantial until early 1962, but by mid-1963, fund reservations of $284 million had been made on applications surviving initial review, loans for $112 million had been approved after detailed analysis of the projects proposed,[68] and $25 million had been disbursed on completed or nearly completed projects. It will be noted from these figures that program lags are moderately long, but given the program's orientation, this is not a serious drawback.

A major problem for the future will be to assist in the development of local resources without impeding the migration of labor to more productive areas. Only careful reviews of project rates of return, in relation to profit rates elsewhere in the country, can ensure success in this respect, but local pressures for the approval of low-rate Area Redevelopment Administration projects might be abated if federal loans were also available on liberal terms to assist people to move from chronic labor surplus areas.

[67] For a description of the procedures followed in setting up these areas see U. S. Department of Commerce, Area Redevelopment Administration, *Annual Report for 1962* (Government Printing Office, 1963), p. 5.

[68] By the Small Business Administration for commercial and industrial loans and by the Housing and Home Finance Agency for public facility loans.

Conclusions

Direct federal lending has painted its postwar stabilization record on a broad canvas but in such complex and subtle colors that different observers receive different impressions. For some it will be the drab greys and blues of missed opportunities and ill-conceived actions that stand out, while others will focus on the bright, vivid streaks recording past successes, and particularly on the rosy glints these project toward the future.

There is no denying that the blues and greys are there, but in assessing their meaning, one should remember that federal loan programs were not established simply to offset fluctuations in private business activity, and that their success, or lack of it, is best judged not in the strictest absolute terms but in relation to the accomplishments of other fiscal and monetary policies, which obviously did not succeed in eliminating either inflation or underemployment from the economic scene.[69] More could have been done, but much was done, however incompletely. Credit terms were varied countercyclically, additional money was provided when unemployment rates were high, and a far-from-fortuitous concentration of liberalizing legislation has materialized at the end of recessions or early in subsequent recoveries.

Nonetheless, there are important problems to be dealt with in the future. The record shows clearly that stabilizing action must be taken early, as soon as a business-cycle turning point can be recognized with reasonable confidence, if the effects are to be felt when they will do the most good. The record also identifies some of the impediments to decisive and timely action: the pleas of government borrowers for stable, or even expanded, public credit during inflationary booms when private money markets are tight; the setting of interest rates by formulas that react to changing economic conditions only with a lag; or the failure to build up, in prosperous times, inventories of approved loan applications that can be released quickly in recession. While these difficulties can all be eliminated, the long time lags, observed above for some of the most important federal loan programs, cannot.

[69] For a highly stimulating, critical evaluation of past policies see J. M. Culbertson, *Full Employment or Stagnation?* (McGraw-Hill, 1964).

It is important, therefore, to consider the size of the impact that the more flexible types of federal lending are capable of exerting. In fiscal 1963, for example, the four major stabilizing programs discussed in the first section of this chapter[70] made disbursements of $1,031 million, received repayments of $617 million and sold loans of $479 million. There was, in short, a negative net credit flow of $65 million. While for reasons given in Chapter 2 it is uncertain that the economic impact was also negative (i.e. deflationary), it seems clear that the programs did not add materially to the growth of national output in that year. Some indication of what might have been done in an expansionary direction may be obtained by taking the postwar peak years of disbursements for each of the four programs (see Appendix A) and combining the figures into one total. This procedure yields gross loan disbursements of $2,119 million, which, if no loan sales had been made, would have produced a positive net credit flow of $1.5 billion in fiscal 1963. This is certainly not a negligible figure, and there is no reason to regard it as a maximum estimate. As for future potentialities in the opposite direction, a drastic cutback in new lending, combined with vigorous attempts to sell part of their existing $5 billion portfolio, would probably enable the programs to generate a negative credit flow of well over $1 billion. By fiscal 1965, for example, their loan repayments are expected to rise to $790 million, and if budget plans are realized, loan sales of $560 million will be made in that year. To achieve a net money inflow of $1.3 billion, therefore, it would be necessary only to balance whatever loan disbursements are made with additional portfolio sales.

I conclude that short-run monetary shifts of considerable magnitude could be brought about by action of the four direct lending programs included in the first section of this chapter. In addition, there is the secondary market program of the Federal National Mortgage Association, which, as argued in the second section, does have as yet unrealized countercyclical potentialities. Its fiscal 1960 mortgage purchases of over $1 billion show what can be done in an expansionary direction, and its $2 billion portfolio (in mid-1963) would permit enough mortgage sales to be made to exert important contractionary effects on

[70] Small business loans, the regular credit programs of the Farmers Home Administration, the special assistance functions of the Federal National Mortgage Association, and the direct housing loans of the Veterans Administration.

private financial markets. Finally, as shown in the third section, even long-lag programs can have some short-run economic impact.[71]

Over the longer period, even more important economic effects can be generated. The programs noted in the preceding paragraph alone would guarantee that, but in addition there are several whose total influence greatly exceeds the amount of federal money needed to finance their lending operations. These include the national defense educational loans dealt with in the fourth section of this chapter, as well as the public works planning and small business investment company programs discussed more briefly in Appendix A.

The postwar record of these federal lending programs, taken as a whole, is far from discouraging. A clearer understanding of their fiscal responsibilities and of their relationships to other programs could make them an important influence in achieving a high and expanding level of economic activity without inflation.

[71] The three major programs discussed—college housing loans, rural electric and telephone loans, and the Eximbank's development project and exporter loans—had a combined peak annual disbursement of $1,169 million.

Major Lending Program Summaries

THIS APPENDIX SUPPLEMENTS Chapter 4 by providing additional information about the direct loan programs there discussed and also by summarizing briefly the pertinent characteristics of five other important programs. Altogether, there are eighteen major programs or agencies, organized into three broad groups (for convenience, the category under which the program was discussed in Chapter 4 is indicated in parentheses):

Marginal Borrower Programs

MB-1 Area Redevelopment Administration (Structural Unemployment)
MB-2 Reconstruction Finance Corporation, Business Loans (Flexible Stabilizer)
MB-3 Small Business Administration, Business Loans (Flexible Stabilizer)
MB-4 Farmers Home Administration (Flexible Stabilizer)
MB-5 Public Facility Loans (Not discussed in Chapter 4)
MB-6 Rural Electrification Administration (Long Lag Program)
MB-7 Small Business Investment and Development Company Loans (Not discussed in Chapter 4)

Unrestricted Programs

U-1 College Housing Loans (Long Lag Program)
U-2 Housing Loans for the Elderly (Long Lag Program)
U-3 Management and Liquidation Functions, Federal National Mortgage Association (Not discussed in Chapter 4)
U-4 Secondary Market Functions, Federal National Mortgage Association (Flexible Stabilizer)
U-5 Special Assistance Functions, Federal National Mortgage Association (Flexible Stabilizer)
U-6 Direct Housing Loans, Veterans Administration (Flexible Stabilizer)
U-7 National Defense Educational Loans (Structural Unemployment)
U-8 Disaster Loans, Reconstruction Finance Corporation and Small Business Administration (Not discussed in Chapter 4)
U-9 Public Works Planning Advances (Not discussed in Chapter 4)

Foreign and Defense Programs

FD-1   Export-Import Bank of Washington (Long Lag Program)

FD-2   Agency for International Development (Long Lag Program)

A number of less important programs are noted at the end of the Marginal Borrower and Unrestricted groups and additional foreign and defense loans are given in Table A-11. The final section, entitled Subsidiary Loan Programs, describes the main kinds of federal direct loans that are made as a more or less incidental byproduct of noncredit spending programs.

The Marginal Borrower and Unrestricted categories were set up, insofar as available data permitted, to reflect a fundamental distinction developed in the analysis of Chapter 2.[1] Ideally, one would like to separate federal borrowers who lack access to private credit from borrowers who simply shift from private to federal loans. In practice, however, one can only distinguish federal programs that are designed *primarily* for marginal borrowers from those that are not. In general, therefore, marginal borrower programs are defined as those whose loans are restricted to applicants unable to obtain private credit "on reasonable terms," in the full knowledge that legislative and administrative interpretations of that phrase vary from one program to another.[2] As a result, the most liberal programs of this type differ only in degree, rather than in kind, from the Unrestricted programs, which typically grant loans to anyone who cannot do as well or better on private credit markets.

The discussion below of each major lending program is divided into six parts:

1. Date of Program Establishment.

2. Loan Characteristics June 30, 1963 (December 31, 1962 in three cases). Basic credit terms and amounts outstanding for the main types of loans made by the agency.

3. Peak Postwar Operational Levels. The highest fiscal-year amounts of loan approvals and disbursements between mid-1946 and mid-1963.

4. Economic Effects. Those program characteristics, such as type of borrower serviced, proposed uses of loan funds and loan-to-value ratios, which determine the strength of the first-round demand-generating effects of the different programs.

5. Stabilization Record. Supplementary material for the agencies discussed in Chapter 4 and brief summaries for the other five programs.

6. Analytical Tables. Deseasonalized time series, loan disbursements by type and other summary data.

[1] Foreign and defense programs were placed in their own group regardless of whether they are restricted to marginal borrowers.

[2] Cf. U. S. Congress, House Banking and Currency Committee, *A Study of Federal Credit Programs*, Vol. 1, pp. 75-91.

Loans Restricted to Marginal Borrowers

MB-1   Area Redevelopment Administration, Department of Commerce
Established May 1961 by 75 Stat. 47.
Loan Characteristics June 30, 1963

	Cumulative Amounts (millions)				
Type of Loan	Initial Approvals[3]	Final Approvals	Disburse-ments	*Interest Rates (percent)*	Maximum Maturity (Years)
Industrial and Commercial					
Urban	$ 69	$29	$ 9	*4*	25
Nonurban	112	40	14	*4*	25
Public Facility	48	43	3	*3⅝*	40
Totals	229	112	25		

Peak Fiscal Year

Initial Approvals	1963	$225 million
Final Approvals	1963	89 million
Net Disbursements	1963	24 million

Economic Effects

Loans are granted to finance the construction of industrial, commercial, and public facilities when funds are not available elsewhere on reasonable terms. According to official estimates the output-generating powers of the loans are at least twice the amount of federal money involved.[4]

MB-2   Business Loans of the Reconstruction Finance Corporation (RFC)
Established June 1934

At mid-1946 direct loans outstanding were $247 million, and the gross amount of deferred participation loans (i.e. both RFC and private bank shares) outstanding was $330 million.

Loan Characteristics June 30, 1963, mostly liquidated. When the RFC was abolished (mid-1957), its remaining business loans were transferred partly to the Small Business Administration, which had liquidated all but $2 million of them by the end of 1962, and partly to the Treasury Department. While business loans cannot be identified in the Treasury's published accounts, at mid-1963 it held only $7 million RFC loans of all kinds.

---

[3] Net of cancellations. Gross initial approvals amounted to $284 million.

[4] U. S. Department of Commerce, Area Redevelopment Administration, *Annual Report 1962,* p. 20.

Peak Fiscal Years

Authorizations	1950	$535 million
Gross Disbursements	1950	302 million
Net Disbursements		
Direct	1950	134 million
Guaranteed	1946	225 million

Economic Effects. In 1947 marginal borrower restrictions were tightened, RFC requiring for the first time proof of the applicant's inability to obtain credit elsewhere on conventional private terms.

Stabilization Record. By its first postwar expansion (guaranteed loans in 1946 and direct loans in 1947), the business program contributed to the general inflation of the period. During 1948, direct loans became increasingly attractive as private interest rates rose, and they expanded again during the 1949-50 recession and recovery, rising from $327 million outstanding at the end of 1948 to $518 million at mid-1950. Outstanding guaranteed loans, however, declined during this period by $70 million. Anti-recession actions were taken in 1949, but Lewis is skeptical of their effectiveness.[5] In any case, the business program did behave countercyclically at this time.

Other RFC loan programs did not play an important expansionary role during the postwar period. Indeed, if all its loans are combined, RFC had a positive net credit flow only during the first half of 1946 ($6 million) and the second half of 1949 ($31 million), and in 1948 its negative flow reached —$164 million. For reasons given in Chapter 2, however, RFC principal repayments probably did not discourage private spending by as much as an equal amount of RFC disbursements stimulated it, and these combined figures should not be taken at face value.

Analytical Tables. Table A-1 summarizes RFC liquidation operations, which in recent years have been divided among the General Service and Small Business Administrations, the Treasury Department, and the Federal National Mortgage Association.

MB-3   Business Loans of the Small Business Administration (SBA)

Established July 1953 by 67 Stat. 230 to begin lending when RFC's lending powers expired September 28, 1953.

Loan Characteristics June 30, 1963, $762 million outstanding, in which SBA's cash investment was $585 million. In general, loans were available at 5½ percent, for a maximum maturity of 10 years and a maximum amount of $350,000. Special terms, however, applied to loans in redevelopment areas (e.g. a 4 percent interest rate) and to "pool" loans made to organized groups of small businesses.

[5] Wilfred Lewis, Jr., *Federal Fiscal Policy in the Postwar Recessions* (Brookings Institution, 1962), pp. 114-15.

Peak Fiscal Year

Gross Disbursements	1962	$260 million
Net Disbursements		
By SBA alone	1962	141 million
By SBA and private lenders	1962	178 million

Economic Effects. See Chapter 4.

Stabilization Record. See Chapter 4.

TABLE A-1. *RFC Liquidation Operations,*
September 28, 1953-June 30, 1962

(Millions of dollars)

Fiscal Year[a]	Amount of Loans Outstanding at End of Year			Reduction During Year in Amount of Loans Outstanding
	Direct	Guaranteed	Total	
1954	$372[b]	$33	$405	—
1955	319	24	343	$ 62
1956	199	12	211	132
1957	143	7	150	61
1958	114	5	119	31
1959	91	3	94	25
1960	65	3	67	27
1961	52	2	54	13
1962	43	0	43	11

Sources: *The Budget of the United States Government,* various years. *Treasury Bulletin;* Small Business Administration, *Semiannual Report,* various years; and Federal National Mortgage Association, *Semiannual Report,* various years; and the *Final Report on the RFC.* Estimates of the gross amounts of RFC-guaranteed loans outstanding were obtained from the Treasury Department, Office of Defense Lending.

  [a] On September 28, 1953, the amounts outstanding were as follows: direct loans, $687 million; estimated gross amount of guaranteed loans, $31 million; loan commitments, $82 million; total RFC credit, $800 million. On June 30, 1954, the amounts outstanding were: direct loans, $436 million; estimated gross amount of guaranteed loans, $33 million; loan commitments, $11 million; total RFC credit, $480 million.

  [b] This figure is less than the corresponding one above on June 30, 1954 by the $64 million of mortgages transferred to FNMA at June 30, 1954 and thereafter indistinguishable from other FNMA mortgage holdings.

Analytical Tables. Table A-2 shows the seasonally adjusted number of business loans received each month from the beginning through mid-1961. The seasonal index used was:

January	77	July	93
February	95	August	105
March	124	September	102
April	103	October	95
May	109	November	91
June	108	December	95

TABLE A-2. *Number of Small Business Administration Business Loan Applications Received, Seasonally Adjusted, 1953-1961*

Date	Number	Date	Number
October 1953	35	August	546
November	75	September	498
December	153	October	529
		November	625
January 1954	240	December	557
February	371		
March	341	January 1958	653
April	364	February	614
May	344	March	692
June	306	April	786
July	318	May	1,008
August	338	June	782
September	346	July	903
October	301	August	874
November	270	September	875
December	298	October	978
		November	924
January 1955	265	December	589
February	236		
March	257	January 1959	979
April	223	February	887
May	225	March	873
June	256	April	870
July	220	May	692
August	260	June	835
September	275	July	732
October	237	August	650
November	273	September	732
December	286	October	671
		November	660
January 1956	347	December	688
February	412		
March	407	January 1960	673
April	407	February	663
May	442	March	685
June	476	April	651
July	437	May	690
August	418	June	841
September	502	July	801
October	728	August	755
November	753	September	758
December	635	October	751
		November	796
January 1957	644	December	817
February	620		
March	566	January 1961	943
April	549	February	756
May	601	March	1,074
June	481	April	1,035
July	557	May	1,109
		June	1,208

MB-4   Farmers Home Administration (FHA), Department of Agriculture
Established. August 1946 by 60 Stat. 1062 to succeed the Farm Security Administration and the Emergency Crop and Feed Loan Division of the Farm Credit Administration. At mid-1946 these agencies had loans outstanding of $604 million.

Loan Characteristics June 30, 1963[6]

Type of Loan	Amount Outstanding June 30, 1963 (Millions)	Interest Rate (Percent)	Term of Maturity (Years)
Operating	$603	5[7]	up to 12[8]
Farm Ownership	341	3–5	10–40
Rural Housing	476	4[7]	10–33
Emergency (Disaster)	86	3[7]	7–20
Soil and water conservation	31	3–5	20–40
Liquidating Programs	14	—	—
Watershed protection and flood prevention	5	Variable[9]	up to 50
Credit sales of real estate	1	5	up to 5

	Peak Fiscal Year	
Direct Loans		
Gross Disbursements[10]	1963	$574 million
Net Disbursements	1963	259 million
Insured Loans		
Authorizations	1963	187 million
Net Disbursements	1963	158 million

Economic Effects. FHA loans are intended for submarginal borrowers, and a 1956 study produced evidence consistent with that hypothesis, showing that FHA customers were typically younger, less wealthy, and had higher debt-to-net-worth ratios than farmers borrowing from commercial banks or the Farm Credit Administration.[11] Operating and emergency loans were most highly concentrated among low-income farmers, with farm ownership loans close behind.

[6] Source of data, U. S. Treasury Department, Fiscal Service, Bureau of Accounts, "Federal Credit Programs of the United States Government, June 30, 1963" (mimeo.).

[7] These rates have remained the same throughout the postwar period.

[8] Initial loans with maturities up to 7 years are renewable for 5 years.

[9] The average interest rate on Treasury borrowings.

[10] Excludes disbursements made by the Agricultural Credit Insurance Fund. In Fiscal 1963 this fund disbursed $186 million but received $170 million from principal repayments and loan sales.

[11] The study was based on a random sample of 25,000 active FHA borrowers out of a total of 177,000. See Russell W. Bierman and Betty A. Case, "The Farmers Home Administration and Its Borrowers," *Agricultural Finance Review*, Vol. 21 (July 1959), pp. 40-67.

The first-round expansionary impact of FHA loans varies with their type. While both rural housing and soil and water conservation loans appear to have been used almost exclusively to purchase new output, in fiscal 1962 19 percent of operating loans and 42 percent of farm ownership loans went to refinance existing indebtedness. Hence, as noted in Chapter 2, they could have been output-generating only in a defensive sense. In addition, 40 percent of 1962 farm ownership loans financed the purchase of existing farms and so had no direct effect on gross national product. Direct farm ownership loans, therefore, have probably not had an important economic impact during the postwar period, but in 1962-63 insured loans of the same kind expanded rapidly (Table A-4).

Stabilization Record. FHA's postwar performance has been marked both by shortages of funds, particularly before 1956, and by frequent program changes, the most important of which through the end of 1961 are summarized below.

	Date	Business Cycle Phase[12]
Interest Rate Increases		
$2\frac{1}{2}$ percent to $3\frac{1}{2}$ per cent	November 1946	E
to 4 percent	June 1948	E
to $4\frac{1}{2}$ percent	September 1954	R
to 5 percent	September 1959	E
Major Program Liberalizations		
Loan restrictions eased	second half 1949	C
Operating loan terms eased	August 1951	E
Soil and water program expanded	August 1954	C/R
Maximum amounts raised; loans for refinancing and to part-time farmers permitted	August 1956	E
Eligibility requirements for farm housing loans relaxed	March 1958	C
Borrower qualifications eased	December 1959	E
Eligibility requirements for farm housing loans relaxed	August 1960	C
Loans to part-time farmers made available everywhere	October 1960	C
Maximum amounts raised; eligibility requirements eased	August 1961	R
New Types of Loans Authorized		
Insured farm ownership	November 1946	E
Farm housing	July 1949	C
Insured soil and water conservation	August 1954	C/R
Direct loans for later conversion into insured loans	August 1958	R
Direct farm enlargement and development, insured loans for domestic farm labor housing	June 1961	R

[12] C = contraction; R = recovery; E = expansion.

Analytical Tables. FHA loans are subject to seasonal fluctuations, the amount outstanding tending to be high at the end of the first quarter of the year and low at the end of the fourth quarter. Analyses were made both of a semiannual series showing the amounts of regular loans outstanding from December 1946 to December 1961 and of a similar quarterly series available only since mid-1953. While the latter showed a relatively stable seasonal pattern of 102-101-101-95 for the four quarters, the former suggested a steadily intensifying fluctuation that was barely perceptible in the late 1940's, but showed a 104-96 pattern a decade later. These results should be regarded as first approximations only since the series used combined several elements—both disbursements and repayments on operating, farm ownership, farm housing, and soil and water conservation loans—which may well have their own separate seasonal variations, and since the quarterly series was available for only a relatively short period of time. It was decided, however, that the potential results of further refinement of the data by type of transaction did not justify the effort involved. Table A-3 gives the seasonally adjusted semiannual series. Table A-4 shows the amount of insured loans authorized and disbursements on direct loans.

TABLE A-3. *Semiannual Changes in the Amount of Regular FHA Loans Outstanding, Seasonally Adjusted at Annual Rates, 1947-1963*[a]

(Millions of dollars)

Period	Amount	Period	Amount
1947-I	$28	1956-I	$ 16
-II	−90	-II	52
1948-I	−26	1957-I	68
-II	−40	-II	66
1949-I	−10	1958-I	44
-II	2	-II	46
1950–I	0	1959-I	60
-II	6	-II	74
1951-I	16	1960-I	48
-II	− 8	-II	118
1952-I	42	1961-I	82
-II	56	-II	206
1953-I	8	1962-I	188
-II	64	-II	234
1954-I	50	1963-I	54
-II	16		
1955-I	−16		
-II	−28		

Source: Unadjusted changes are given in Table B-5.

[a] Direct operating, farm ownership, rural housing, and soil and water conservation loans.

TABLE A-4. *Farmers Home Administration, Amount of Insured Loans Authorized and Disbursements on Direct Loans, by Type and Fiscal Year, 1946-1963*

(Millions of dollars)

Fiscal Year	Amount of Disbursements on Direct Loans						Amount of Insured Loans Authorized
	Operating	Farm Owner-ship	Soil and Water Conser-vation	Rural Housing	Disaster	Total	
1946	$ 83	$23	$1	—	$ 1	$107	—
1947	90	47	2	—	—	139	—
1948	60	21	1	—	—	82	$ 2
1949	76	18	2	—	3	99	8
1950	85	19	3	$ 13	35	155	17
1951	103	20	4	26	20	173	18
1952	110	22	5	22	33	191	10
1953	120	20	6	20	44	210	11
1954	140	19	6	16	93	274	10
1955	122	19	4	0	89	235	47
1956	138	19	2	1	86	245	48
1957	180	26	5	21	67	299	33
1958	174	46	4	30	64	318	27
1959	187	28	3	61	40	318	37
1960	199	27	3	43	24	296	18
1961	232	32	3	58	26	351	26
1962	275	34	4	106	62	482	150
1963	300	21	8	183	62	574	187
Totals	2,673	461	66	600	750	4,549	649

Sources: Farmers Home Administration, Budget and Statistics Division, and *The Budget of the United States Government*, various years.

MB-5   Public Facility Loans, Housing and Home Finance Agency (HHFA)
    Established August 1955 by 69 Stat. 642.
    Loan Characteristics June 30, 1963
    Amount Outstanding—$104 million
    Interest Rates—based on statutory formula (see Table A-5)
    Maximum Maturity—40 years.
    Peak Fiscal Year

Authorizations	1963	$60 million
Gross Disbursements	1963	33 million
Net Disbursements	1963	29 million

TABLE A-5. *Interest Rates on Public Facility Loans, 1955-1964*
(Percent)

Time Period	Interest Rate	
	General Obligation Bonds	Revenue Bonds
Oct. 3, 1955–Sept. 3, 1956	3.75	4.25
Sept. 4, 1956–Nov. 16, 1956	3.875	4.375
Nov. 17, 1956–June 20, 1957	4.00	4.50
June 21, 1957–Nov. 3, 1957	4.25	4.75
Nov. 4, 1957–Jan. 19, 1958	4.50	5.00
Jan. 20, 1958–May 27, 1958	4.125	4.625
May 28, 1958–Sept. 23, 1958	4.00	4.375
Sept. 24, 1958—Feb. 22, 1960	4.50	4.875
Feb. 23, 1960–May 17, 1960	4.75	5.00
May 18, 1960–July 17, 1960	4.625	4.875
July 18, 1960–Nov. 20, 1960	4.50	4.75
Nov. 21, 1960–Feb. 1, 1961	4.375	4.625
Feb. 2, 1961–June 30, 1961	4.125	4.375
	Loans in Redevelopment Areas	Loans in All Other Areas
July 1, 1961–June 30, 1962	3.375	3.625
July 1, 1962–June 30, 1963	3.50	3.75
July 1, 1963–June 30, 1964	3.625	3.875

Source: U. S. Housing and Home Finance Agency, Community Facilities Administration, and *The Budget of the United States Government*, various years.

Economic Effects. Loans finance the construction of local public works, such as water, sewage, and gas distribution systems, and are granted only when credit is not available elsewhere on reasonble terms. In general, HHFA has defined "reasonable interest rates" as those that all public agencies eligible for federal loans would have to pay on private credit markets.[13] Program time lags appear to be moderately long. Loans to small communities for the construction of basic public works have priority over other types, but this rule has been relaxed in each of the last two recessions.

Stabilization Record. Prior to mid-1961 interest rates were both flexible and reasonably well coordinated with monetary policy.[14] Note in Table A-5, for example, the three reductions during the 1960-61 recession. In mid-1961,

[13] U. S. House Banking and Currency Committee, *A Study of Federal Credit Programs* (Government Printing Office, 1964), Vol. 1, pp. 80-81 and Vol. 2, p. 520.

[14] Procyclical fluctuations, however, have not been completely absent. Under the tight money conditions of fiscal 1959, for example, loan operations were higher than under the easier monetary conditions of fiscal 1961. *Ibid.*, Vol. 2, p. 532.

a more important reduction was made (¾ percent), but since then rates have been changed only once a year. Late in both the 1957 and the 1960 recessions eligibility restrictions were relaxed as a deliberate countercyclical policy. The effects were apparently significant—according to official estimates the $55 million inflow of applications in 1958 would otherwise have been only $32 million.[15] Loan approvals in 1961 were $38 million compared to only $21 million in 1960. But most of the economic impact must have occurred toward the end of the recovery period or even later. Loans outstanding, for example, did not show significant increases until the second quarter of 1959 in the first case and until the first quarter of 1962 in the second (Table B-5). Finally, it may be noted that in the Housing Act of 1961, Congress, perhaps under the influence of high unemployment, enacted a major liberalization of the program, lowering interest rates, increasing funds, relaxing eligibility requirements and authorizing mass transportation loans for the first time.[16]

MB-6   Rural Electrification Administration (REA), Department of Agriculture

Established

Electric loans in May 1935; $454 million outstanding at mid-1946.
Telephone loans in October 1949 by 63 Stat. 948.

Loan Characteristics June 30, 1963

Amounts outstanding
   $2,960 million electric
   $733 million telephone
Interest rate 2 percent.
Maximum maturity 35 years.

Principal and interest payments may be deferred up to 5 years on electric and up to 3 years on telephone loans.

Maximum loan-to-value ratios: 100 percent on electric; 90 percent on telephone.

Peak Fiscal Years

Approvals		
Electric and combined	1949	$449 million
Telephone	1961	143 million
Gross Disbursements		
Electric	1949	321 million
Telephone	1961	108 million
Combined	1963	332 million

[15] U. S. Housing and Home Finance Agency, *Twelfth Annual Report, 1958* (Government Printing Office, 1958), p. 251.

[16] For further details see U. S. Housing and Home Finance Agency, *Fifteenth Annual Report, 1961*, pp. 266-67.

Net Disbursements

Electric; combined	1961	299 million
Telephone	1961	99 million

Economic Effects. Loans are almost entirely output-generating, electric loans approved in fiscal 1962 being used 40 percent for distribution facilities, 38 percent for generating plants, 22 percent for transmission lines and 1 percent for the purchase of consumer electric facilities. In the same year, telephone loans approved were used 53 percent for new construction, 38 percent for improvements, 6 percent for acquisitions, and 3 percent for refinancing.[17] Indirect stimulating powers may also be high, REA studies indicating, for example, that for every dollar its borrowers invest in electric distribution facilities, consumers served by these borrowers spend four dollars for new wiring, appliances, and equipment.[18]

While applicants for electric and telephone loans are not required to prove their lack of access to private lenders,[19] there is ample evidence that they could in fact have obtained only limited amounts of money in this way.[20]

Stabilization Record. In spite of its relative inflexibility (Chapter 4), the program has been affected by short-run fiscal policies. In early 1953, REA was directed by the Budget Bureau to slow down operations because of general budgetary pressures, and then later in the year the developing recession induced an acceleration in administrative procedures by as much as 50 percent.[21] Again in early 1958, REA borrowers were urged to speed up their activities, and maximum maturities on loans to finance consumer electric facilities were raised. These loans, however, have never been an important part of the program. Amounts approved in the three fiscal years 1957, 1958, and 1959 were $5.4, $3.9, and $3.2 million respectively.

Analytical Tables. Seasonal analyses of semiannual loan applications were made and yielded indexes of 119-81 for electric loans and 111-89 for telephone loans. Seasonally adjusted series are given in Table A-6.

[17] Rural Electrification Administration, *Report of the Administrator* (1962).

[18] *Department of Agriculture Appropriations for 1960,* Hearings before the House Appropriations Committee (Government Printing Office, 1959), Pt. 3, p. 1681.

[19] Section 5 loans, which finance the purchase of electrical appliances and equipment and have not been an important part of the total program, are granted only to those who cannot obtain funds elsewhere on reasonable terms.

[20] See, for example, George S. Tolley, "The Rural Electrification Administration," in the Commission on Money and Credit *Federal Credit Agencies* (Prentice-Hall, 1963), pp. 385-434, and U. S. House Banking and Currency Committee, *A Study of Federal Credit Programs,* Vol. 2, pp. 16 and 36.

[21] Rural Electrification Administration, *Report of the Administrator, 1954,* p. 38, and *Department of Agriculture Appropriations for 1956,* Hearings before the House Appropriations Committee (Government Printing Office, 1955), Vol. 1, p. 1455.

TABLE A-6. *Amounts of REA Electric and Telephone Loan Applications Received, Seasonally Adjusted at Annual Rates, 1953-1961*
(Millions of dollars)

Period	Electric	Telephone
1953-II	$199	$ 64
1954-I	132	71
-II	168	43
1955-I	197	66
-II	213	86
1956-I	193	68
-II	384	73
1957-I	382	98
-II	323	106
1958-I	197	90
-II	200	137
1959-I	252	111
-II	295	107
1960-I	347	149
-II	158	134
1961-I	264	74

Source: Rural Electrification Administration.

MB-7   Small Business Investment and Development Company Programs

Established August 1958 by 72 Stat. 689.

Loan Characteristics June 30, 1963

Amounts Outstanding

Small business investment company debentures	$91 million
Small business investment company loans	32 million
State and local development company loans	27 million

Terms, investment companies, 5 percent, 20-year maximum terms with principal repayments postponable until the second half of the loan term; development companies, 5-5½ percent, 25-year maximum terms. Special 4 percent rate in areas of substantial unemployment and in redevelopment areas.

Peak Fiscal Year

Gross Disbursements	1963	$74 million
Net Disbursements	1963	67 million

Economic Effects. The program was established to fill an important private credit gap by stimulating and supplementing the flow of equity capital and long-term loans to small businesses. After the stock market break of May 1962, it was reportedly the only major source of such funds.[22] SBA loans are made to small business investment and local development companies only when private funds are unavailable on reasonable terms, and each applicant must furnish satisfactory evidence to this effect.[23] State development companies, however, need only certify that the money requested from SBA is not otherwise available.

Since SBA investment and development company loans provide only part of the funds needed and used by the borrower, both are capable of stimulating additional, and even multiple, amounts of private lending. At the end of 1962, for example, when SBA's investment in them was less than $100 million, small business investment companies had outstanding loans of $360 million and a total capitalization of $553 million.[24] While it cannot be argued that none of this activity would have taken place without government assistance, it seems highly likely that $100 million underestimates the true impact of the program. Similarly, SBA provides no more than half of a state development company's funds, and it requires all aided local development companies to finance at least 20 percent of project costs.

Stabilization Record. Though the founding of the small business investment company program may not be entirely independent of the high rate of unemployment that prevailed during most of the preceding year,[25] it is not likely to play an important role in future countercyclical fiscal policy, since SBA exercises only indirect, regulatory control over the institutions that authorize the loans to small business. Indeed, the more effective the program becomes, the less need there should be for SBA's business loans which, as shown in Chapter 4, can be used effectively for short-run economic stabilization.

MB-8 Other Marginal Borrower Programs

At mid-1963 there were two small, direct loan programs for marginal borrowers in the Interior Department; and two loan insuring agencies, both for

[22] U. S. House Banking and Currency Committee, *A Study of Federal Credit Programs,* Vol. 2, p. 824.

[23] *Ibid.,* pp. 816-22, 838-39.

[24] Small Business Administration, *1962 Annual Report to the President and Congress,* pp. 29-30.

[25] A front page *Wall Street Journal* story of March 19, 1958, for example, attributed to the recession a heightening of interest in a similar program to be financed by the Federal Reserve Banks.

marginal borrowers in the transportation sector of the economy, had made direct loans in connection with their default proceedings. Together, however, the four had direct loans of only $55 million outstanding in mid-1963:

Bureau of Indian Affairs Loan Fund (Interior Department)	$18 million
Fisheries Loan Fund (Interior Department)	6 million
Federal Ship Mortgage Insurance Fund (Commerce Department)	16 million
Railroad loan guaranties (Interstate Commerce Commission)	15 million

Five other programs were under liquidation during part or all of the post-war period: the Home Owners' Loan Corporation, from the beginning when it held loans of $874 million; the Federal Farm Mortgage Corporation, from mid-1947 when it had loans of $131 million; HHFA's prefabricated and Alaska housing programs, from 1953-54 when they held loans of $7 and $13 million respectively; and the Federal Reserve Board's Section 13b industrial working capital loans, from 1958 when less than $500,000 were outstanding.

Unrestricted Loans

U-1   College Housing Loans, Housing and Home Finance Agency

Established April 1950 by 64 Stat. 77.

Loan Characteristics June 30, 1963

Fund reservations in fiscal 1963	
College housing	$245 million
College service facilities	34 million
Housing for student nurses and interns	9 million
Loans outstanding at end of fiscal 1963	1,476 million

Maximum maturity 50 years.

Interest rate[26] $3\frac{1}{2}$ percent in fiscal 1963

Peak Fiscal Years

Authorizations 1962	$380 million
Gross Disbursements 1963	305 million
Net Disbursements 1963	288 million

Economic Effects. Housing bonds are offered for sale on the open market, and HHFA purchases whatever part of each issue is not taken by private investors at equally favorable (or better) terms. HHFA estimates that on the average the program has financed 60 percent of the total financial needs of colleges and universities for housing and related facilities. A compilation of bond issues of public institutions of higher learning for such facilities showed

---

[26] See Stabilization Record below.

that, between January 1950 and March 1963, $716 million were awarded to HHFA, $253 million were sold to other investors after having first been filed with HHFA, and $525 million were sold directly to other investors.[27] Since many of the HHFA-assisted colleges could, and would, have obtained funds elsewhere, though on more stringent credit terms,[28] the program has added an indeterminate amount of liquidity to private loan markets.

Stabilization Record. Long and variable time lags restrict the usefulness of the program for short-run stabilization (Chapter 4), but construction was accelerated after February 1961 as a deliberate antirecessionary policy. There is no simple adjustment that can convert available statistical series into good measures of the economic effects of college housing loans as far as timing goes. But the two series given below, in which loan approvals have been shifted forward one year and disbursements back one-half year to allow for average program lags, may provide a useful first approximation to what is desired. One encouraging aspect, in any case, is the close correlation between the movements of the two series.[29]

Fiscal Year	Adjusted Loan Approvals	Adjusted Loan Disbursements
1953	$ 23 million	$ 20 million
1954	62	33
1955	27	27
1956	42	61
1957	111	110
1958	199	181
1959	265	229
1960	180	163
1961	180	220
1962	330	308
1963	380	—

The major liberalization of the program made in August 1955 (69 Stat. 644) indicated the sensitivity of loan demand to a reduction in interest rates. Between fiscal 1955 and 1956 the inflow of applications jumped from 116 to 388, and loan approvals rose from $42 million to $111 million. Interest rates that have prevailed under the program are as follows:

[27] U. S. House Banking and Currency Committee, *A Study of Federal Credit Programs,* Vol. 2, pp. 475-78.

[28] *Ibid.,* pp. 478-79.

[29] Sources of data: through 1961, from the Housing and Home Finance Agency, Community Facilities Administration. After 1961, data are from HHFA, *Housing Statistics.*

Period	Rate
July 1, 1951–April 30, 1952	$2\frac{3}{4}$ percent
May 1, 1952–April 30, 1953	3
May 1953	$3\frac{1}{2}$
June 1953	3

Fiscal Year	
1954	$3\frac{1}{2}$
1955	$3\frac{1}{4}$
1956	$2\frac{3}{4}$
1957	$2\frac{7}{8}$
1958	3
1959	$2\frac{7}{8}$
1960	$3\frac{1}{8}$
1961	$3\frac{1}{2}$
1962	$3\frac{3}{8}$
1963	$3\frac{1}{2}$
1964	$3\frac{5}{8}$

U-2 Housing Loans for the Elderly, Housing and Home Finance Agency

Established September 1959 by 73 Stat. 654.

Loan Characteristics and Peak Operations

Table A-7 summarizes the development of the program through mid-1963. Maximum maturity of loans, 50 years.

Interest rates, same as those under college housing program.

TABLE A-7. *Housing Loans for the Elderly, Quarterly, 1960-1963*

(Millions of dollars)

Year and Quarter	Applications Received	Net Fund Reservations	Net Loan Agreements Executed (Approvals)	Loans Outstanding at End of Quarter
1960-4	$44[a]	$ 3		
1961-1	18	5	$ 1	
1961-2	51	8	1	
1961-3	55	8	3	$ 0.3
1961-4	34	13	12	1.5
1962-1	48	22	4	2.7
1962-2	37	8	10	4.9
1962-3	26	5	7	6.9
1962-4	21	25	4	11.5
1963-1	23	23	9	16.8
1963-2	29	29	18	23.2
Total	386	149	69	—

Sources: U. S. Housing and Home Finance Agency, *Housing Statistics,* and U. S. Treasury Department, *Treasury Bulletin.*

[a] From the beginning of the program.

Economic Effects. Like college housing loans, these are available to all borrowers who are unable to obtain funds elsewhere on equally favorable terms. They finance the construction of rental housing and related facilities and are designed for elderly persons whose incomes are too high to qualify them for public housing but too low to support the rental of ordinary private housing.

Stabilization Record. Too new a program to have one, but Table A-7 indicates that time lags are relatively long.

U-3 Management and Liquidation Functions, Federal National Mortgage Association

Established November 1954, by 68 Stat. 613, to liquidate the mortgage lending program then superseded by the Special Assistance and Secondary Market Funds.

Loan Characteristics June 30, 1963

Amounts Outstanding

FHA Mortgages	$513 million
VA Mortgages	619 million
Defense Housing Corporation	30 million
Public Housing Corporation	108 million

Peak Fiscal Years

Net Disbursements

Pre-1954	1950	$592 million
Post-1954	1960	—476 million

Economic Effects. When it was established, the Management and Liquidation Fund was instructed to dispose of its mortgage holdings "in an orderly manner, with a minimum of adverse effect upon the home mortgage market and minimum loss to the Federal Government" (68 Stat. 613). Taken literally, this would have meant no mortgage sales at all, except in the unlikely circumstance of a perfectly elastic demand for home mortgages on the part of private lenders. As Table A-8 shows, sales have not in fact been extensive, apart from a special operation in 1960 to be discussed below. The mortgages held are unattractive to private lenders because they carry low interest rates (4 percent and 4½ percent) and are small enough in amount to make the costs of handling them relatively high.[30] In recent years, however, the administration has become increasingly interested in higher sales, largely to permit tax reduction without undue curtailment of expenditure programs.[31]

[30] Cf. *Continuation of Present Debt Ceiling*, Hearing before the House Ways and Means Committee (Government Printing Office, 1963), pp. 66-71, where the salability of federally held financial assets is discussed at length.

[31] Discussed in Chap. 2, pp. 42-44, and Chap. 3, pp. 77-78. The 1965 Budget, for example, proposed that Congress authorize the sale of certificates of participation in pools of mortgages held by FNMA and the Veterans Administration. See *The Budget of the United States Government, Fiscal Year Ending June 30, 1965,* App., p. 751.

TABLE A-8. *Portfolio Reductions by the FNMA Management and Liquidation Fund, Semiannually, 1955-1963*

(Millions of dollars)

Period	Reduction in the Amount of Mortgages Held		
	By Repayments and Other Credits	By Net Sales[a]	Total
1954 (November and December)	22	−88	−66
1955-I	79	−202	−123
-II	91	− 62	29
1956–I	79	− 19[b]	60
-II	88	− 10[b]	78
1957-I	68	− 7[b]	61
-II	67	0	67
1958-I	71	0	71
-II	91	3	94
1959-I	93	1	94
-II	96	0	96
1960-I	69	311	380
-II	67	0	67
1961-I	67	5	72
-II	79	0	79
1962-I	81	10	91
-II	72	5	77
1963-I	60	9	69
Total	1,340	−44[c]	1,296

Source: FNMA, *Semiannual Reports; Treasury Bulletin.*

[a] Total sales minus total purchases. Purchases from other federal agencies have been excluded as intragovernmental transfers.

[b] Mortgage sales were suspended from October 1955 to June 1958, and these figures consequently are made up entirely of purchases.

[c] Total sales were $370 million and total purchases $414 million.

Stabilization Record. Performance before 1954 was discussed in Chapter 4. Since then, the program has on several occasions reacted to other fiscal developments. In 1957-58, the fund was used to help the Treasury bypass the statutory debt ceiling,[32] and in 1959, it played a prominent role in the

[32] See Marshall A. Robinson, *The National Debt Ceiling: An Experiment in Fiscal Policy* (Brookings Institution, 1959).

tightly balanced administrative budget submitted by the Eisenhower Administration for 1960 (the estimated surplus was only $70 million). Careful readers of that document soon discovered a novel plan to trade $335 million of FNMA-held VA mortgages for an equal amount of outstanding, nonmarketable Treasury securities.[33] This transaction, it was officially argued, would hasten the liquidation of FNMA's pre-1954 portfolio without exerting an adverse effect on the home mortgage market; but other observers, many of them Democrats, preferred to stress the fact that without the mortgage-bond swap, the 1960 budget would show a deficit of $265 million. In addition, since the government was planning to trade 4 percent mortgages for 2¾ percent bonds maturing in 1975-80, there was an obvious risk that the Treasury would suffer substantial losses of net income.

After much discussion and some delay, the plan was carried out, and during the first half of 1960, $311 million of 4 percent mortgages were exchanged for $316 million of 2¾ percent Treasury bonds. In the event, then, private investors gained higher-yielding, slightly riskier securities[34] but lost in the process, probably, some of their desire to buy other home mortgages. Whatever economic effects there were, they were not of major proportions, but the whole controversy highlighted some of the anomalies of budget accounting discussed in Chapter 2.

U-4   Secondary Market Functions, Federal National Mortgage Association
Established November 1954 by 68 Stat. 613.
Loans Outstanding December 31, 1962
FHA Mortgages, $1,717 million
VA Mortgages, $1,129 million
Peak Fiscal Years
Net Purchases 1960, $1,097 million
Net Sales 1963, $605 million
Economic Effects, see Chapter 4.
Stabilization Record, see Chapter 4.

U-5   Special Assistance Functions, Federal National Mortgage Association
Established November 1954 by 68 Stat. 613.
Loan Characteristics December 31, 1962, see Table A-9.
Peak Fiscal Years
Net Purchases, 1959, $1,057 million
Net Sales, 1963, $193 million

Economic Effects. Purchases are confined to selected types of mortgages (Table A-9) which, though not readily marketable at the time, are expected to become so in the future. FNMA is currently free, by setting its purchase prices, to decide exactly how unmarketable its eligible mortgages should be,

---

[33] *The Budget of the United States Government for the Fiscal Year Ending June 30, 1960* (Government Printing Office, 1959), pp. M53 and 303.

[34] Since the mortgages were VA-guaranteed, the risks were not great.

but in recent years its prices have been close to market levels. On the other hand, for many of its acquisitions there may be little prospect of their soon becoming generally acceptable to private investors.[35] To concentrate its impact on new construction, FNMA buys only FHA and VA mortgages that were insured or guaranteed within the preceding four months.

TABLE A-9. *Active Programs Under FNMA Special Assistance Functions at the End of 1962*

(Millions of dollars)

Program[a]	Authorized by the President (P) or by Congress (C)	Program Authorization	Net Contracts Executed by December 31, 1962	Total Purchases Made by December 31, 1962
Urban renewal	P	875	698	542
Armed services	C	500	476	474
Cooperative housing	C	225	217	197
Elderly persons	P	251	192	98
Below market interest rate housing	P	380	64	17
Alaska	P	58	58	57
Other[b]	P	37	9	1
Total	P	1,601	1,020	715
Total	C	725	693	671

Source: Housing and Home Finance Agency, *Sixteenth Annual Report, 1962*, p. 246.

[a] Ranked in order of the amount of net contracts executed.

[b] Disaster, Guam, Consumer Cooperative, Experimental housing, and Restricted Indian Lands Programs.

Stabilization Record. The main features are discussed in Chapter 4. Because of legislatively determined minimums, purchase prices were both inflexible and relatively high between August 1956 and August 1958. Since then FNMA has had complete discretion, which it used countercyclically to make three price reductions during the fall of 1959 and three price increases in the spring of 1961. In fiscal 1963, the program was a major participant in the government's extensive sale of financial assets. The agency has noted a tendency for its operations to respond to monetary conditions, contracting when they are easy and expanding when they are tight.[36]

[35] For a discussion of these, and other, aspects of FNMA's special assistance operations, see Jack M. Guttentag's study of the agency in Commission on Money and Credit, *Federal Credit Agencies* (Prentice-Hall, 1963), especially pp. 114-23. See also U. S. House Banking and Currency Committee, *A Study of Federal Credit Programs,* Vol. 2, p. 645.

[36] *Ibid.,* p. 656.

U-6   Direct Housing Loans, Veterans Administration

Established April 1950 by 64 Stat. 75.

Loan Characteristics June 30, 1963

Amounts Outstanding

Home Loans, $1,261 million

Vendee Loans, $14 million

Interest Rate Range 5¼ percent–6 percent

Maximum Maturity 30 years.

Peak Fiscal Year

Gross Disbursements 1960, $281 million

Net Disbursements 1960, $229 million.

Economic Effects. The loans are restricted to veterans living in rural areas where federally guaranteed or insured loans are not generally available from private lenders, but there is no requirement that applicants be unable to obtain conventional private loans. Neither VA direct nor VA-guaranteed loans, in other words, are restricted to marginal borrowers.

Direct loans may be used to purchase either new or existing houses, and VA estimates show that through 1959 63 percent of the funds advanced financed new construction.

Stabilization Record. Beginning in 1955 a concerted effort was made, by means of the Voluntary Home Mortgage Credit Program (VHMCP), to substitute federally insured private mortgages for direct VA home loans. That the effort was successful in fiscal 1956 may be judged from the following:

Fiscal Year	Number of Loans Placed Under Voluntary Home Mortgage Credit Program	Veterans Administration Gross Loan Disbursements
1955	2,100	$117 million
1956	15,800	92 million
1957	13,000	117 million

As a result, VA's uncommitted funds increased from less than $20 million in mid-1955 to $121 million in mid-1957, with the favorable effects during the following recession already noted in Chapter 4.

Two important, end-of-recession, legislative liberalizations were made in the program:

1. 72 Stat. 73, April 1, 1958, provided additional funds, increased the maximum loan size from $10,000 to $13,500, authorized advance loan commitments to builders, and directed that the referral of VA applicants to VHMCP should no longer hold up VA's processing and review.

2. 75 Stat. 201, July 6, 1961, gave the program its first extended period of unchallenged existence (until mid-1976); ample funds were authorized, and the maximum loan size was raised to $15,000.

From the outset VA has been authorized to sell its loan paper but not at prices below par (unpaid principal plus accrued interest). As a result only

$84 million had been sold by mid-1962, but sales were $181 million in fiscal 1963, and to raise this still further the administration presented legislation (H.R. 6652) that would authorize sales at whatever prices the VA Administrator determines to be reasonable.

U-7 National Defense Educational Loans, Department of Health, Education, and Welfare

Established September 1958 by 72 Stat. 1580.

Loan Characteristics June 30, 1963

Type	Amount Outstanding	*Interest Rate (Percent)*	Maturity
Student Loans	$291 million	3	10 years
Section 207 Loans to Institutions	2 million	$3\frac{1}{8}$–$4\frac{1}{4}$	15 years
Section 305 Loans to Nonprofit Schools	2 million	$3\frac{3}{8}$–$3\frac{5}{8}$	10 years

Peak Fiscal Years

Net federal disbursements 1963, $90 million

Funds advanced to students 1963, $104 million

Economic Effects. Student loans are discussed in Chapter 4. Section 207 loans are granted to colleges and universities unable to finance on reasonable terms their own 10 percent contribution to the Student Loan Funds. They are, consequently, marginal borrower loans, but the limited availability of information about them has necessitated their inclusion in the unrestricted category in several of the Appendix B tabulations. Because few Section 207 loans have been made, this procedure has virtually no effect on the totals involved.

Section 305 loans are designed to raise the quality of instruction in private, nonprofit elementary and secondary schools. So far, however, the program has not been important, and only 10 percent of the funds available have been borrowed. In fiscal 1962, loans for $672,000 were approved, and were to be used 73.9 percent for science, 25.8 percent for modern foreign languages, and 0.3 percent for mathematics (the three authorized purposes).[37]

Stabilization Record. The program is too new to have one. It may have some built-in flexibility, more young people tending to go to college (and hence to need national defense loans) when jobs are hard to get than when the economy is booming. On the other hand, economic adversity is hardly the most auspicious occasion for the undertaking of personal indebtedness, particularly since repayment of the loans has to begin one year after the recipient's education is completed, regardless of how much or how little he is then earning. Only the future can tell which of these opposing tendencies will predominate.

[37] U. S. Department of Health, Education, and Welfare, *Report on the National Defense Education Act, Fiscal Years 1961 and 1962* (Government Printing Office, 1963), pp. 17 and 73.

U-8   Disaster Loans, Reconstruction Finance Corporation and Small Business Administration

Established March 1933, transferred to SBA on September 28, 1953.

Loan Characteristics December 31, 1962

Amounts Outstanding

RFC, $0.9 million

SBA, Direct, $76.3 million

SBA, Guaranteed, $0.4 million

Type of SBA Loan	Amount Authorized in Calendar 1962	*Interest Rate* (*Percent*)	Maximum Maturity
Physical damage resulting from natural catastrophes	$26.3 million	3	20 years
Drought and excessive rainfall	0.6 million	3	20 years
Businesses displaced by federally aided construction projects	6.8 million	$3\frac{1}{2}$	20 years

Unlike small business loans there is no maximum loan amount.

Peak Fiscal Years, 1952 for the RFC program, when $22 million was authorized and $14 million disbursed; 1956 for the SBA program, when $44 million was authorized and $33 million disbursed.

Economic Effects. Physical-damage loans, the oldest type, are used to repair or replace tangible property lost in a natural disaster. Drought loans, authorized in 1955, and excessive rainfall loans, authorized in 1958, may be used for working capital, to replenish normal inventories, or to cover debt repayments that the borrower would have been able to make on his own had the disaster not occurred. Displaced business loans, authorized in 1961, assist the relocation of small business firms, and the interest rate on them is set at 1/4 percent above the average interest rate on all interest-bearing federal debt.

Emergency loans are designed to provide limited amounts of public assistance to businessmen whose operations have been unfavorably affected by the weather or by the federal government itself. Applicants for them are not required to establish their inability to obtain private loans. For these reasons, the program has been separated from other SBA credit operations and placed in the Unrestricted Loan group. It should be noted, however, that SBA does not in practice grant disaster loans to anyone for whom it has reliable evidence of his access to sufficient private funds on reasonable terms.[38]

Stabilization Record. Not relevant because of the special nature of the loans.

U-9   Public Works Planning Advances, Housing and Home Finance Agency

Established August 1954 by 68 Stat. 590. This is the third such program, the

[38] U. S. House Banking and Currency Committee, *A Study of Federal Credit Programs,* Vol. 2, p. 810.

first existing from October 1944 to mid-1947 and the second from October 1949 to October 1951.

Loan Characteristics June 30, 1963. Loans are interest-free advances granted to state and local governments to plan public works and are normally repayable when construction is started. At mid-1963, $30 million were outstanding.

Peak Fiscal Year, 1963 when disbursements of $12.5 million were made and repayments of $7.0 million received.

Economic Effects. The program is designed (1) to combat recession by encouraging the development and maintenance of a shelf of planned public works on which construction can be begun quickly, and (2) to fill a credit gap created by the inability of many communities to borrow money for planning before they have found construction funds, which in turn are difficult to obtain without detailed project plans.

Planning advances involve little federal money (only $34.5 million[39] through fiscal 1963), but they may stimulate the construction of a much greater volume of public works. Exactly how much cannot be determined, and one can only note the distressingly wide range between the min-max estimates of the program's output-generating powers. For the former, total federal disbursements were $51 million through fiscal 1963; and for the latter, the estimated construction costs of all planning projects approved through calendar 1962 were $4.5 billion.[40] Loan repayments, which were $21.6 million through fiscal 1963, can be used as an indirect measure of the amount of construction begun (a multiplier of 50 should yield a conservative estimate of total costs),[41] and increases in the amount of advances outstanding should indicate how rapidly the shelf of public works projects is being built up. If the net amount of advances outstanding is taken as an accurate indicator of those that will be repaid in the future, the shelf of plans was $19.5 million in mid-1963, representing total construction costs, say, of nearly $1 billion.

Even if the present program were terminated, its economic impact would continue for some time. Construction costs of projects started under the second program before its lending powers were ended, for example, were only $100 million, compared to $426 million during the next three years and another $210 million in the seven years after that (Table A-10).

[39] Budget expenditures of $30.5 million, as shown for the Public Works Planning Fund, plus appropriations for salaries and expenses of $4 million, shown separately.

[40] U. S. Housing and Home Finance Agency, *Sixteenth Annual Report, 1962,* p. 262.

[41] In September 1962, however, the Public Works Acceleration Act (76 Stat. 541) waived the repayment of advances on all projects initiated under its provisions. Thereafter, consequently, repayments will underestimate the volume of construction starts.

TABLE A-10. *Estimated Construction Costs of Projects Started Under the First and Second Advance Planning Programs, 1947-1961*

(Millions of dollars)

Year	First Program	Second Program	Total
1947	$110[a]		$110
1948	227		227
1949	220		220
1950	265	$ 7	272
1951	151	96[a]	247
1952	84	148	232
1953	83	119	202
1954	83	159	242
1955	42	40	82
1956	103	27	130
1957	26	50	76
1958	39	42	81
1959	42	19	61
1960	22	21	43
1961	16	11	27
Total	1,513	739	2,252

Sources: U. S. Housing and Home Finance Agency, *Tenth Annual Report, 1956* (Government Printing Office, 1957), pp. 289-90. Figures for later years were computed from cumulative data given in subsequent annual reports.

[a] Authority to approve new advances ended in this year.

Stabilization Record. The program was inaugurated as part of the Eisenhower Administration's 1954 antirecession program, but the inflow of repayments so far indicates steady growth rather than a high sensitivity to business cycles.

Fiscal Year	Amount of Repayments (Millions)	Predominant Cyclical Phase[42]
1957	$0.1	E
1958	1.2	C
1959	2.1	R
1960	3.7	E
1961	3.2	C
1962	4.3	R
1963	7.0	E

Construction starts under the second program, however, did expand countercyclically in 1954 (Table A-10), and there seems little doubt that the present

[42] E = expansion; C = contraction; R = recovery.

program has materially increased the stabilizing powers of state and local public works spending.

U-10   Other Unrestricted Loan Programs
Four other programs need be noted only briefly.

	Amounts Outstanding June 30, 1963
Default and vendee loans of the VA loan guaranty program	$355 million
Vendee loans of the Federal Housing Administration	349 million
Treasury Department loans to the District of Columbia for capital outlays	104 million
Interior Department loans to finance Alaska public works	17 million

Default loans occur when a veteran fails to meet the payments on his VA-guaranteed home loan, and the Veterans Administration, believing that there is a reasonable prospect that he will be able to meet his financial commitments eventually, takes the mortgage over from the private lender, thereby converting it to a direct loan. More frequently, however, the VA acquires the security behind the defaulted loan; and then later, in the process of selling the home, it typically extends its credit to the buyer in the form of a vendee loan. FHA vendee loans arise in a similar way. Both agencies have expanded these loans at an increasing rate during most of the postwar period, the peak increases in loans outstanding occurring in the VA series in fiscal 1960 ($84 million) and in the FHA series in fiscal 1962 ($90 million). In 1963, however, loan sales produced the first decline ($106 million) in the VA Loan Guaranty Fund's portfolio.

Foreign and Defense Loans

Table A-11 summarizes the state of direct federal lending in the foreign and defense area at mid-1963. The first program, that of the Export-Import Bank of Washington, was established in 1934 to promote United States exports. This has remained its basic goal although some of its loans have been made with the needs of national security in mind. Unlike the other major lending agencies, Eximbank's peak postwar net credit flow of $957 million occurred at the very beginning of the period (fiscal 1947), the only recent year to approach it being fiscal 1959 when the Bank's net disbursements were $473 million. Since then, gross disbursements of over $2.3 billion have failed to match loan repayments and sales, and by mid-1963 the Bank's outstanding portfolio had declined by $164 million.

Table A-12 shows Eximbank gross disbursements by type since 1954. As noted in Chapter 4, both development project and exporter loans are subject to long and variable time lags, and neither commodity nor emergency foreign trade loans can be counted on to be fully, or even primarily, output-generating. As a result, the program has not been a major short-run stabilizer.

TABLE A-11. *Amounts of Direct Foreign and Defense Loans Outstanding at June 30, 1963, by Major Group and Type of Loan*

(Millions of dollars)

Major Foreign Lending Programs	$9,419
Export-Import Bank	
Development Loans	1,896
Exporter Loans	111
Emergency Foreign Trade	1,289
Agency for International Development	
Development Loans—Dollar	801
—Foreign Currency	967
Mutual Security Loans—Dollar	1,647
—Foreign Currency	2,629
Private Enterprise Loans—Foreign Currency	79
Other Foreign Loans	4,062
United Kingdom loan	3,205
Finland loan	5
Postwar Economic Assistance Agreements	
Germany, February 27, 1953	200
Japan, January 9, 1962	462
Military Assistance Credit Sales	185
Maritime Administration Credit Ship Sales	5
Major Defense Loans	76
Expansion of Defense Production	64
Defense Production Guarantee Program	12
Other Defense Loans	125
Interior Department, Office of Minerals Exploration	11
State Department, United Nations Loans	113
Treasury Department, Civil Defense Loans	1

Sources: Treasury Department, Fiscal Service, Bureau of Accounts, *Federal Credit Programs of the United States Government, June 30, 1963* (mimeo.). Treasury Department, *Treasury Bulletin* (November 1963), pp. 105-43. Interior Department, *Annual Report for Fiscal 1963.*

A similar judgment is appropriate for the other types of loans listed in Table A-11, though for different reasons. Both AID foreign aid loans and defense production credits, for example, were extended to further the achievement of United States foreign policy objectives, which bear no relationship to domestic stabilization needs. Several of the other programs have been in liquidation during most of the postwar period. Among the smaller programs is one with the unusual feature of risk-sharing between borrower and lender. Searchers for strategic minerals who lack access to private loans on reasonable terms can apply to the Office of Minerals Exploration for advances covering

TABLE A-12. *Export-Import Bank of Washington, Loan Disbursements by Major Type, 1954-1963*

(Millions of dollars)

Fiscal Year	Type of Loan			
	Development Project	Exporter	Commodity	Emergency Foreign Trade
1954	$105	$ 6	$ 52	$280
1955	107	2	—	45
1956	122	9	55	—
1957	145	24	61	—
1958	334	30	150	332
1959	440	16	41	212
1960	324	33	17	47
1961	439	22	41	24
1962	425	107	10	361
1963	450	11	1	46

Source: *The Budget of the United States Government,* various years.

up to half of their total costs, and these advances are repayable with interest only if the exploration is successful. In less fortunate cases, the federal government and the private enterpriser share the losses between them. Between April 1951, when the program began, and mid-1962, the Office of Minerals Exploration spent $15 million on successful ventures and had received repayments of $4 million from them. Another $9 million had been advanced without prospect of recovery.

Subsidiary Loan Programs

In mid-1963 the federal government had almost $1.2 billion outstanding in the form of loans made as an incidental feature of various nonlending expenditure programs.

Federal Savings and Loan Insurance Corporation	$ 47 million
Life insurance policy loans	566 million
Public Housing Administration	94 million
Urban Renewal Administration	129 million
Reclamation project, distribution systems, and rehabilitation and betterment loans	67 million
Storage facility and equipment loans	71 million
Vendee loans	207 million
	$1,181 million

All of these loans, subordinate as they are to other activities, lie outside the mainstream of fiscal policy making. For purposes of this study, consequently, only their general nature needs to be noted.

1. As insurer of savings deposits in savings and loan associations, the Federal Savings and Loan Insurance Corporation must deal with those associations that find themselves in financial difficulties; and to minimize bankruptcies and liquidations, the corporation extends loans whenever the recipient's future prospects are sufficiently favorable.

2. The Veterans Administration provides life insurance under four different funds—the National Service Life, United States Government Life, Service-Disabled Veterans, and Veterans Special Term Insurance Funds—and as a result makes policy loans to insured veterans.

3. Both the Public Housing and Urban Renewal Administrations, whose activities are too well-known to require description here, make direct loans to local government agencies participating in their programs. These temporary advances are then replaced by federally guaranteed private loans, which eventually are repaid to a large extent by the federal government itself.[43]

4. Since 1955-56 the Interior Department's Bureau of Reclamation has supplemented its own construction activities with loans to nonfederal organizations to finance both the construction and the rehabilitation of small reclamation projects and irrigation distribution systems.

5. The Commodity Credit Corporation's storage facility loans arose directly from the agricultural price-support programs and the great need they created for the storage of surplus crops. Private expansion of such facilities is encouraged partly by guaranteed occupancy contracts and partly by direct loans to defray construction costs.

6. Finally, vendee loans have been granted to the purchasers of a wide variety of government assets, including surplus war goods, merchant ships, the RFC synthetic rubber and tin facilities, atomic energy installations, and property of the Inland Waterways Corporation and the Tennessee Valley Authority.

[43] For an analysis of these credit activities see George F. Break, *The Economic Impact of Federal Loan Insurance* (National Planning Association, 1961), Chap. 6.

General Tables

Sources

1. Treasury Department, "Corporations and Certain Other Business-Type Activities: Statements of Financial Condition," published quarterly in the *Treasury Bulletin.*

2. Treasury Department, "Corporations and Certain Other Business-Type Activities: Income and Expense; Source and Application of Funds," published semiannually in the *Treasury Bulletin.*

3. Treasury Department, *Federal Credit Programs of the United States Government,* mimeographed for each fiscal year.

4. "Special Analysis of Federal Credit Programs," published annually in *The Budget of the United States Government.*

5. "Detailed Estimates for Federal Funds and Trust Funds," published annually in the Appendix to *The Budget of the United States Government.*

6. U. S. Office of Business Economics, *Foreign Grants and Credits for the United States Government,* published quarterly.

7. Lending agency semiannual and annual reports and supplementary data obtained directly.

(Please turn the page for tabulations)

TABLE B-1. *Federal Direct Loan Programs Included in Basic Tables*

Agency and Program	Designation Used in Later Tables	Period Covered by Program[a]
A. Loans Restricted to Marginal Borrowers		
Major Programs		
Farmers Home Administration—		
Regular Loans	FHA/R	BE
Emergency Loans	FHA/E	BE
Rural Electrification Administration—		
Electric Loans	REA/E	BE
Telephone Loans	REA/T	bE
Reconstruction Finance Corporation—		
Business Loans	RFC/B	Be
Other Loans	RFC/O	Be
Small Business Administration—		
Business Loans	SBA/B	bE
Investment and Development Company Loans	SBA/IDC	bE
Housing and Home Finance Agency—		
Public Facility Loans	HHFA/PF	bE
Other Programs		
Farmers Home Administration—		
Direct Loans Made by Agricultural Credit Insurance Fund		bE
Area Redevelopment Administration		bE
Direct Loans Made by Federal Ship Mortgage Insurance Fund		bE
Bureau of Indian Affairs, Interior Department		BE
Fisheries Loan Fund, Interior Department		bE
Direct Loans by Virgin Islands Corporation		bE
Interstate Commerce Commission—Direct Loans Made Under Railroad Loan Guarantee Program		bE

[a] B = beginning of the postwar period, June 30, 1946.
  E = end of period of study, June 30, 1963.
  b = beginning of loan program (used when program was started during the postwar period).
  e = end of active life of the loan program (i.e. the beginning of liquidation) when this occurred during the period of study.
  o = program completely liquidated by June 30, 1963.
  x = data not available back to the beginning of the program.
  y = program merged with other programs, and hence indistinguishable from them thereafter.

TABLE B-1 *(Continued)*

Agency and Program	Designation Used in Later Tables	Period Covered by Program[a]
Federal Reserve Board—Section 13b Working Capital Loans		Bo
Housing and Home Finance Agency—		
Alaska Housing Loans		be
Prefabricated Housing Loans		be
B. Unrestricted Loans		
Major Programs		
Federal National Mortgage Association—		
Original Program	FNMA/OP	Be
Secondary Market Operations Fund	FNMA/SMF	bE
Special Assistance Functions Fund	FNMA/SAF	bE
Housing and Home Finance Agency—College Housing Loans	HHFA/CH	bE
National Defense Educational Loans to Students	NDEA/SL	bE
Veterans Administration—Direct Home Loans	VA/DHL	bE
Emergency Loans by the Reconstruction Finance Corporation and the Small Business	RFC/E	Be
Administration[b]	SBA/E	bE
Vendee Loans by the Federal Housing Administration	FHA/V	BE
Veterans Administration	VA/V	bE
Other Programs		
Treasury Department—Loans to the District of Columbia		bE
Housing and Home Finance Agency—		
Public Works Planning Advances, First and Second Programs		xe
Public Works Planning Advances, Third Program		bE
Housing Loans for the Elderly		bE
Interior Department—Alaska Public Works Loans		xE
National Defense Educational Loan Program—		
Loans to Institutions and Nonprofit Schools		bE
RFC Mortgage Company		Be

[b] In some tables these programs are included in the "other" category.

TABLE B-1 (*Continued*)

Agency and Program	Designation Used in Later Tables	Period Covered by Program[a]
C. Foreign and Defense Loans		
Major Programs		
Agency for International Development—		
Program Loans	AID/P	bE
Development Loans	AID/D	bE
Export-Import Bank of Washington	EIB	BE
Direct Loans Made for the Expansion of Defense Production and Under the Defense Production Guarantee Program	DPL	bE
Foreign Currency Loans Made to Private Enterprises ("Cooley" Loans)	CL	bE
Other Foreign Programs		
Treasury Department—		
United Kingdom Loan		BE
World War I Loan to Finland		BE
1953 German Loan Agreement		cE
Other Single Country Loans		xE
Reconstruction Finance Corporation—Loans to United Kingdom and the Philippines		Bo
Loans to Poland, the European Coal and Steel Community and Peru		bE
Deficiency and Basic Materials Development Loans		bE
Defense Department—Military Assistance Credit Sales		xE
Surplus Property Credit Sales		xE
Lend-Lease Agreements Converted to Loans		cE
Occupied Area Commodity Credits		Bo
Other Defense Programs		
Interior Department—Office of Minerals Exploration		bE
Public Health Service—Hospital and Community Facility Loans		xE
State Department—Emergency Loans to Individuals		xE
Treasury Department—		
Civil Defense Loans		bE
Refugee Loans		bE
General Services Administration—Section 303 Advances		bo

TABLE B-1 *(Continued)*

Agency and Program	Designation Used in Later Tables	Period Covered by Program[a]
Office of Education—World War II Student Loans		Bo
State Department—Loans to the United Nations		bE
Defense Department—Direct Contractor Loans		Bo
Housing and Home Finance Agency—		
War Public Works Loans		xo
Defense Community Facility Loans		by
Defense Homes Corporation		BE
General Services Administration—Federal Facilities Corporation: Liquidation of Vendee Loans		by
Reconstruction Finance Corporation—Smaller War Plants Corporation		By
D. Subsidiary Direct Loans		
Public Housing Administration—Temporary Direct Loans	PHA	BE
Urban Renewal Administration—Temporary Direct Loans	URA	bE
Commodity Credit Corporation—Storage Facility Loans	CCC/SF	bE
Interior Department—Bureau of Reclamation Loans	DI/BR	bE
Veterans Administration—Life Insurance Policy Loans	VA/LIF	BE
Federal Savings and Loan Insurance Corporation Loans	FSLIC	bE
Vendee Loans—		
Maritime Administration Ship Sales and Construction Loans	V/MA	BE
General Services Administration—Surplus Property Credit Sales	V/GSA	bE
Federal Facilities Corporation Credit Sales	V/FFC	be
Housing and Home Finance Agency Community Disposal Operations Fund	V/CDOF	bE
Public Housing Administration Purchase Money Mortgages	V/PHA	bE

TABLE B-1 *(Continued)*

Agency and Program	Designation Used in Later Tables	Period Covered by Program[a]
E. Domestic Direct Loans Under Liquidation		
Major Programs		
Reconstruction Finance Corporation—		
Financial Institution and Public Works Administration Loans	By	
Other Loans	bE	
Federal National Mortgage Association—		
Management and Liquidation Fund	bE	
Home Owners Loan Corporation	Bo	
Public Works Administration	BE	
Federal Farm Mortgage Corporation	bE	
RFC Mortgage Company	by	
Other Programs		
Housing and Home Finance Agency—		
Alaska Housing Loans	by	
Prefabricated Housing Loans	by	
Public Agency Loans	by	
Public Works Planning Advances	bE	
Inland Waterways Corporation	bE	
Agricultural Marketing Revolving Fund	Bo	
Tennessee Valley Authority	Bo	
Loans to Railroads	Bo	

TABLE B-2. *Amounts of Direct Federal Loans Outstanding at Mid-1946 and Mid-1963, by Major Group*

(Millions of dollars)

Major Group	June 30, 1946	June 30, 1963
Marginal Borrower Programs	1,577	6,170
Unrestricted Programs	46	7,753
Foreign and Defense Programs		
Major	601	9,495
Other	278	4,182
Subsidiary Programs	512	1,181
Domestic Liquidating Programs	1,216	1,393
Total	4,230	30,174

TABLE B-3. *Changes in the Amounts of Direct Federal Loans Outstanding by Program Group, by Fiscal Year, 1947-1963, Semiannually, 1946-1962*

(Millions of dollars)

Period	Marginal Borrowers	Unrestricted	Foreign and Defense		Subsidiary	Domestic Liquidating	Total	
			Major	Other			Semiannual	Fiscal Year
1946-II	− 16	− 1	458	640	0	−126	955	
1947-I	155	59	499	1,443	6	−162	2,000	2,955
1947-II	107	3	226	1,428	219	− 58	1,925	
1948-I	117	45	270	230	202	− 88	776	2,701
1948-II	143	148	45	− 74	− 4	− 81	177	
1949-I	154	266	728	0	− 9	−142	997	1,174
1949-II	241	367	105	3	− 1	−140	575	
1950-I	179	232	174	− 71	27	−184	357	932
1950-II	49	297	84	− 54	60	−100	336	
1951-I	161	301	183	− 45	110	− 42	668	1,004
1951-II	23	346	118	− 13	134	− 24	584	
1952-I	64	251	388	− 1	4	− 36	670	1,254
1952-II	97	218	197	−101	299	− 20	690	
1953-I	125	316	103	108	−286	− 10	356	1,046
1953-II	74	36	326	− 93	− 88	− 61	194	
1954-I	173	− 89	−111	− 15	−296	−195	−533	−339
1954-II	17	188	71	− 32	− 62	− 37	145	
1955-I	134	84	89	19	23	104	453	598
1955-II	− 19	159	59	−157	1	−107	− 64	
1956-I	175	229	138	− 68	19	−102	391	327
1956-II	50	519	103	−170	38	−109	431	
1957-I	247	771	63	−180	48	− 83	866	1,297
1957-II	112	664	475	−118	43	− 75	1,101	

TABLE B-3 *(Continued)*

Period	Program Group						Total	
	Marginal Borrowers	Unrestricted	Foreign and Defense		Subsidiary	Domestic Liquidating	Semiannual	Fiscal Year
			Major	Other				
1958-I	215	42	273	− 88	8	− 83	367	1,468
1958-II	92	416	577	−134	31	−102	880	
1959-I	292	1,221	405	−231	− 19	−105	1,563	2,443
1959-II	103	1,083	8	−136	27	− 97	988	
1960-I	236	1,036	340	− 67	41	−240	1,346	2,334
1960-II	117	667	254	−129	51	− 72	888	
1961-I	258	− 41	491	−702	7	− 75	− 62	826
1961-II	218	731	595	− 10	77	−100	1,511	
1962-I	376	355	418	− 30	78	− 96	1,101	2,612
Fiscal 1963	611	−706	532	12	9	−151		307

TABLE B-4. *Amounts of Direct Federal Loans Outstanding at the End of Selected Postwar Quarters, Marginal Borrower Programs*

(Millions of dollars)

Quarters	Business Cycle Phase[a]	FHA/R	FHA/E	REA/E	REA/T	RFC/B[b] SBA/B	RFC/o[b] SBA/ IDC	HHFA/ PF	Other[c]	All Loans
1946-2	—	604	4	454		247	261		7	1,577
1948-4	P	523	2	1,000		327	221		8	2,081
1949-4	T	514	7	1,302		481	160		10	2,474
1950-2	R/E	524	32	1,414		518	154		12	2,654
1953-2	P	590	55	1,982	32	369	106		38	3,172
1954-3	T	652	102	2,132	68	7			13	2,974
1955-3	R/E	646	110	2,206	110	22			12	3,106
1957-3	P	728	105	2,393	241	125		2	25	3,619
1958-2	T	767	106	2,472	302	183		11	22	3,863
1959-2	R/E	829	74	2,584	390	289	0	32	49	4,247
1960-2	P	892	55	2,706	480	341	8	46	58	4,586
1961-1	T	969	52	2,773	556	383	25	53	57	4,868
1961-4	R/E	1,040	46	2,833	626	454	54	62	66	5,181
1963-2	—	1,420	91	2,960	733	585	150	104	127	6,170

[a] P = peak; T = trough; R/E = transition from recovery to expansion.
[b] RFC through 1953-2; SBA thereafter.
[c] For list of programs see Table B-1.

TABLE B-5. *Amounts of Direct Federal Loans Outstanding at the End of Selected Postwar Quarters, Unrestricted Programs*

(Millions of dollars)

Quarters	Business Cycle Phase[a]	HHFA /CH	RFC/E[b] SBA/E	FNMA/ OP[c] FNMA/ SMF	FNMA/ SAF	NDEA /SL	FHA/ V	VA/V	VA/ DHL	Other[e]	All Loans
1946-2	—		1	6			22[d]			17	46
1948-4	P		3	199			22	1		34	259
1949-4	T		5	828			20	4		33	890
1950-2	R/E		4	1,056			20	7		36[d]	1,123
1953-2	P	15	16	2,498			37	40	207	1	2,814
1954-3	T	59	1	2,364			46[d]	53	315	2	2,840
1955-3	R/E	84	12[d]	30			62[d]	64	393	2	647
1957-3	P	237	42[d]	1,445	39		112[d]	119	572	10	2,576
1958-2	T	374	48	1,394	164		127	159	692	14	2,972
1959-2	R/E	555	49	1,574	1,211		144	235	821	20	4,609
1960-2	P	758	43	2,600	1,690	71	167	321	1,050	44	6,744
1961-1	T	895	46	2,770	1,800	128	192[d]	371	1,184	54	7,440
1961-4	R/E	1,054	57	2,872	1,881	176	236	444	1,301	80	8,101
1963-2	—	1,476	81	2,138	1,612	291	349	369	1,261	176	7,753

[a] P = peak; T = trough; R/E = transition from recovery to expansion.
[b] RFC through 1953-2; SBA thereafter.
[c] Original program through 1954-3; Secondary Market Fund thereafter.
[d] Interpolated.
[e] For list of programs see Table B-1.

TABLE B-6. *Amounts of Direct Federal Loans Outstanding at the End of Selected Postwar Quarters, Major Foreign and Defense Programs*

(Millions of dollars)

Quarters	Business Cycle Phase[a]	Programs					All Loans
		AID/P	AID/D	EIB	DPL	CL	
1946-2	—			601			601
1948-4	P	83		2,016			2,099
1949-4	T	853		2,079			2,932
1950-2	R/E	964		2,143			3,107
1953-2	P	1,530		2,514	139		4,183
1954-3	T	1,562		2,648	175		4,385
1955-3	R/E	1,722		2,580	219		4,521
1957-3	P	2,084		2,578	244		4,906
1958-2	T	2,412	2	2,987	247		5,648
1959-2	R/E	2,874	67	3,460	219	11	6,631
1960-2	P	3,244	262	3,231	209	31	6,977
1961-1	T	3,511	435	3,330	199	43[b]	7,518
1961-4	R/E	3,720	695	3,683	155	64	8,317
1963-2	—	4,276	1,768	3,296	76	79	9,495

[a] P = peak; T = trough; R/E = transition from recovery to expansion.
[b] Interpolated.

TABLE B-7. *Amounts of Direct Federal Loans Outstanding at the End of Selected Quarters, Subsidiary Programs, Loans Made in Connection with Noncredit Spending Programs*

(Millions of dollars)

Quarters	Business Cycle Phase[a]	Programs						Totals
		PHA	VA/LIF	CCC/SF	URA	DI/BR	FSLIC	
1946-2	—	278	115[b]					393
1948-4	P	285	126					411
1949-4	T	285	140	5				430
1950-2	R/E	305	146	8				459
1953-2	P	604	198	20	22			844
1954-2	T	198	220	25	32			475
1955-2	R/E	99	245	33	37			414
1957-2	P	94	302	23	49			468
1958-2	T	91	340	22	69			522
1959-2	R/E	89	378	31	71	15		584
1960-2	P	93	426	44	73	18	30	684
1961-2	T	98	477	47	79	35	45	781
1961-4	R/E	95	498	69	101	44[b]	45	852
1963-2	—	94	566	71	129	67	47	974

[a] P = peak; T = trough; R/E = transition from recovery to expansion.
[b] Interpolated.

TABLE B-8. *Amounts of Direct Federal Loans Outstanding at the End of Selected Quarters, Subsidiary Programs, Vendee Loans*

(Millions of dollars)

Quarters	Business Cycle Phase[a]	Programs					All Loans
		V/MA	V/GSA	V/PHA	V/FFC	V/CDOF	
1946-2	—	119					119
1948-4	P	486		11			497
1949-4	T	442	228[b]	12			782
1950-2	R/E	412	243	16			671
1953-2	P	356	162	31			549
1954-2	T	321	134	55			510
1955-2	R/E	286	117	91	20		514
1957-2	P	270	59	172	10	6	517
1958-2	T	235	64	184	10	11	504
1959-2	R/E	207	70	168	9	5	459
1960-2	P	178	76	1[c]	8	8	271
1961-2	T	148	82	1	7	4	242
1961-4	R/E	138	102	1	[d]	4	245
1963-2	—	110	93	1	[d]	4	208

[a] P = peak; T = trough; R/E = transition from recovery to expansion.
[b] Interpolated.
[c] Most of the loans were transferred to FNMA's Management and Liquidation Fund.
[d] Included in V/GSA column.

TABLE B-9. *Semiannual and Quarterly Changes in the Amounts of Direct Marginal Borrower Loans Outstanding, by Major Program, 1946-1963*

(Millions of dollars)

Quarters	All Loans	FHA /R	FHA /E	REA /E	REA /T	RFC /B	RFC /O	SBA /B[a]	SBA /IDC[a]	HHFA /PF	Other Loans[b]
1946-3+4	−16	−16		74		−16	−57				−1
1947-1+2	155	14		102		31	6				2
-3+4	108	−45		105		44	4				0
1948-1+2	116	−13		120		− 2	11				0
-3+4	143	−20		144		23	− 5				0
1949-1+2	154	0		154		58	−58				0
-3+4	241	−10	7	148		96	− 3				2
1950-1+2	179	11	22	112		38	− 6				2
-3+4	26	− 8	−12	130		−83	− 4				3
1951-1+2	161	19	11	101		28	− 6				9
-3+4	23	−14	−12	96	2	−44	−11				6
1952-1+2	64	32	23	83	6	−54	−29				2
-3+4	97	17	−14	80	9	17	4				−15
1953-1+2	125	21	28	79	15	−14	− 3				− 1
-3	51	11	1	42	7	−14	4				0
-4	23	− 3	− 7	29	5	—	—				− 1
1954-1	123	49	41	26	8						− 2
-2	50	1	14	26	8			2			− 1
-3	41	3	− 3	27	9			5			− 1
-4	−24	−21	−33	16	10			5			− 1
1955-1	103	31	43	16	10			3			0
-2	31	−13	8	23	10			3			0
-3	20	− 3	−12	19	12			4			0
-4	−39	−36	−38	19	13			4			0
1956-1	122	43	39	19	12			8			0
-2	53	− 4	15	18	17			8			0
-3	43	2	−11	21	15			14			1
-4	7	−14	−33	20	18			14			2

[a] Interpolated from semiannual data.
[b] For list of programs included see Table B-1.

TABLE B-9 *(Continued)*

Quarters	All Loans	FHA /R	FHA /E	REA /E	REA /T	RFC /B	RFC /O	SBA /Bᵃ	SBA /IDCᵃ	HHFA /PF	Other Loansᵇ
1957-1	174	72	24	38	19			18		0	3
-2	73	2	7	23	19			18		0	4
-3	81	18	− 8	29	19			17		1	4
-4	31	−27	−25	34	19			17		3	10
1958-1	144	51	26	26	19			21		5	− 3
-2	71	16	0	19	22			21		2	− 9
-3	72	5	−10	28	20			24		3	2
-4	20	−28	−36	29	24			24		2	5
1959-1	171	68	16	24	21			29		3	10
-2	121	17	− 3	31	23			29	0	13	10
-3	85	8	− 3	32	23			14	1	5	5
-4	18	−36	−23	30	24			14	1	4	4
1960-1	159	77	9	38	19			12	3	2	0
-2	77	14	− 1	22	24			12	3	3	0
-3	91	23	− 4	26	24			14	5	2	1
-4	26	−35	−12	24	27			14	5	2	1
1961-1	165	89	13	18	24			14	8	3	− 3
-2	93	28	2	15	23			14	8	3	0
-3	123	49	− 3	19	22			28	10	3	− 5
-4	95	− 6	− 5	25	25			29	10	3	14
1962-1	245	114	29	31				42	14	9	7
-2	131	24	12	35				42	15	4	3
-3	146	71	−12	38				16	18	5	10
-4	61	− 3	−23	37				16	18	10	6
1963-1	255	110	31	58				7	15	9	25
-2	148	63	7	35				7	15	5	16

TABLE B-10. *Semiannual and Quarterly Changes in the Amounts of Direct Unrestricted Loans Outstanding, by Major Program, 1946-1963*

(Millions of dollars)

Quarters	All Loans	HHFA /CH	FNMA/OP[a] SMF	FNMA /SAF	NDEA /SL	FHA /V[b]	VA/V	VA /DHL	Other Loans[e]
1946-3+4	− 1		− 1			3			−3
1947-1+2	59		− 1			0			60
-3+4	3		− 1			−1			5
1948-1+2	45		47			−2			0
-3+4	148		148			−1	1		0
1949-1+2	266		265			−1	1		1
-3+4	367		364			0	2		1
1950-1+2	232		227			0	3		2
-3+4	297		291			0	4		2
1951-1+2	301		232			3	6	59	1
-3+4	346		271			6	6	53	10
1952-1+2	251	1	218			3	6	20	3
-3+4	218	4	174			2	5	32	1
1953-1+2	316	9	256			2	6	43	0
-3	79	6	42			1	3	26	1
-4	− 43	8	− 78			1	2	24	0
1954-1	− 59	10	− 96			2	4	21	0
-2	− 30	10	− 65			2	3	20	0
-3	93	9	63			2	2	16	1
-4	95	6	70			2	2	14	1
1955-1	37	6	1[d]			4	2	22	2
-2	47	10	8[d]			4	3	20	2
-3	61	3	20			5	4	23	6
-4	98	7	56			5	4	20	6
1956-1	109	8	70	0		5	5	10	9
-2	120	13	78	0		5	5	10	9
-3	165	15	118	2		8	6	13	9
-4	354	19	297	4		8	6	17	3

[a] Original program through 1954; Secondary Market Fund thereafter.

[b] Interpolated from semiannual data, 1953-1961.

[e] Includes RFC and SBA emergency loans. For other programs see Table B-1.

[d] Secondary Market Fund only. During the first half of 1955 mortgage holdings of the Management and Liquidation Fund increased by $123 million. This amount is included in Table B-12 under Domestic Liquidating Programs.

TABLE B-10 *(Continued)*

Quarters	All Loans	HHFA /CH	FNMA/OP[a] SMF	FNMA /SAF	NDEA /SL	FHA /V[b]	VA/V	VA /DHL	Other Loans[c]
1957-1	458	28	382	8		5	8	24	4
-2	313	34	217	11		5	8	34	3
-3	314	28	197	14		9	11	52	3
-4	350	36	190	33		9	12	67	3
1958-1	232	48	82	47		2	14	36	3
-2	−190	53	−324	45		2	14	17	3
-3	70	40	− 60	45		5	16	22	2
-4	345	36	47	209		5	17	29	2
1959-1	581	39	83	402		3	18	35	1
-2	639	66	110	391		3	24	43	2
-3	596	60	203	272		5	22	34	0
-4	486	68	273	86		6	18	35	0
1960-1	491	32	321	62		5	21	50	0
-2	544	44	230	60	71	6	22	110	1
-3	404	57	206	46	23	8	20	41	3
-4	262	32	96	43	15	8	15	50	3
1961-1	26	47	−133	21	19	9	14	43	6
-2	− 68	64	−248	29	0	9	23	38	17
-3	276	47	83	28	48	17	23	27	3
-4	454	50	266	25	0	17	25	52	19
1962-1	350	44	151	23	26	20	22	32	32
-2	3	90	−151	3	0	36	2	0	23
-3	105	82	− 23	− 23	46	9	−12	15	11
-4	115	74	− 1	5	4	20	−25	18	20
1963-1	−280	61	−319	− 74	39	18	−19	4	10
-2	−648	71	−390	−204	0	10	−46	−111	22

TABLE B-11. *Semiannual Changes in the Amounts of Direct Foreign and Defense Loans Outstanding, by Major Program, 1946-1962*

(Millions of dollars)

	Major Programs					
		AID and Predecessors		Defense Production Loans	Total Major Programs[a]	Other Programs[b]
Period	Eximbank	Program Loans	Development Loans			
1946-II	458				458	640
1947-I	499				499	1,443
-II	226				226	1,428
1948-I	270				270	230
-II	− 38	83			45	− 74
1949-I	29	699			728	0
-II	34	71			105	3
1950-I	64	110			174	− 71
-II	10	74			84	− 54
1951-I	116	57		10	183	− 45
-II	− 24	116		26	118	− 13
1952-I	104	246		38	388	− 1
-II	112	57		28	197	−101
1953-I	52	15		36	103	108
-II	287	7		32	326	− 93
1954-I	−128	7		10	−111	− 15
-II	− 24	80		15	71	− 32
1955-I	− 9	68		12	71	19
-II	− 36	75		20	59	−157
1956-I	9	119		10	138	− 68
-II	− 7	109		1	103	−170
1957-I	− 27	89		1	63	−180
-II	359	111		5	475	−118
1958-I	51	218	2	2	273	− 88
-II	318	270	4	−17	577	−134
1959-I	155	191	61	−11	405	−231
-II	−260	169	92	− 5	8	−136
1960-I	31	201	103	− 4	340	− 67
-II	15	119	117	− 4	254	−129
1961-I	122	273	135	−48	491	−702
-II	315	84	181	− 2	595	− 10[c]
1962-I	−116	317	227	−14	418	− 30[c]

[a] Total for major programs includes foreign currency loans made to private enterprises (Cooley loans) not shown separately in Table.
[b] For list of programs included see Table B-1.   [c] Estimated.

TABLE B-12. *Subsidiary and Domestic Liquidating Programs, Semi-annual Changes in the Amount of Loans Outstanding, 1946-1962*[a]

(Millions of dollars)

Period	Subsidiary Loans	Domestic Liquidating Programs
1946-II		−126
1947-I	6	−162
-II	219	− 58
1948-I	202	− 88
-II	− 4	− 81
1949-I	− 9	−142
-II	− 1	−141
1950-I	27	−184
-II	60	−100
1951-I	110	− 42
-II	134	− 24
1952-I	4	− 36
-II	299	− 20
1953-I	−286	− 10
-II	− 88	− 61
1954-I	−296	−195
-II	− 62	− 37
1955-I	23	104
-II	1	−107
1956-I	19	−102
-II	38	−109
1957-I	48	− 83
-II	43	− 75
1958-I	8	− 83
-II	32	−102
1959-I	− 18	−105
-II	28	− 97
1960-I	42	−240
-II	52	− 72
1961-I	8	− 75
-II	78	−100
1962-I	80	− 96

[a] For list of programs included see Table B-1.

TABLE B-13. *Major Loans Under Liquidation During the Postwar Period, Amounts Outstanding at the Beginning and End*

(Millions of dollars)

Loan Agency or Program	Beginning Date[a]	Amounts Outstanding at	
		Beginning	June 30, 1963
Home Owners' Loan Corporation	Dec. 31, 1945	874	—
Public Works Administration	Dec. 31, 1945	148	61
Reconstruction Finance Corporation			
Financial Institution Loans	Dec. 31, 1945	310	[b]
Foreign Loans	Dec. 31, 1945	251	—
Public Works Administration Securities	Dec. 31, 1945	72	[b]
Other Loans	June 30, 1953	580	7[c]
Reconstruction Finance Corporation Mortgage Company	June 30, 1947	69	[b]
Federal Farm Mortgage Corporation	June 30, 1947	131	1
Federal National Mortgage Association Management and Liquidation Fund	Dec. 31, 1954	2,435	1,271
United Kingdom Loan	June 30, 1948	3,750	3,205

[a] The nearest half-year date for programs beginning liquidation during the postwar period.
[b] Merged with other loans.
[c] Loans administered by the Treasury Department. Other RFC loans not separately identifiable.

TABLE B-14. *Amounts of Gross Disbursements Made by Major Direct Lending Programs, by Fiscal Year, 1947-1963*

(Millions of dollars)

Fiscal Year	FHA	REA	RFC	SBA	HHFA /CH	VA /DHL	EIB	AID	NDEA /SL	PHA	URA	VA /LIF	DPL
1947	139	190	194				1,085			1			
1948	82	246	139				599			48			
1949	99	321	188				214	782		26		100	
1950	155	287	308				196	182		19		107	
1951	173	268	215			60	227	132		223	2	122	11
1952	191	235	91		1	84	244	361		622	7	118	70
1953	210	232	148		14	89	516	73		924	17	122	84
1954	274	210	18	2	35	111	443	14		526	24	126	83
1955	235	196		25	32	117	154	148		215	30	99	57
1956	245	209		62	33	92	185	194		237	20	86	45
1957	299	259		94	98	117	230	210		250	32	103	16
1958	318	288		126	167	209	846	369		204	39	119	30
1959	318	305		178	185	180	709	596	10	149	69	127	16
1960	296	321		147	210	281	421	600	50	132	127	118	12
1961	351	291		191	211	244	526	734	71	132	110	125	7
1962	482	293		348	246	207	903	1,036	89	171	157	126	23
1963	574	332		293	305	196	508	1,438	104	379	143	115	15
Total	4,441	4,483	1,301	1,466ᵃ	1,537	1,987	8,006	6,869	324	4,258	777	1,713	469

[a] $154 million of this amount was for emergency loans.

176

TABLE B-15. *Amounts of Mortgages Purchased and Sold by the Federal National Mortgage Association, by Fiscal Year, 1948-1963*

(Millions of dollars)

Fiscal Year	Original Program and Secondary Market Fund		Special Assistance Functions Fund	
	Purchases	Sales	Purchases	Sales
1948	47	0		
1949	424	0		
1950	946	311		
1951	855	272		
1952	605	40		
1953	586	60		
1954	481	560		
1955	610	201		
1956	229	3	0	0
1957	1,037	5	24	0
1958	581	393	146	0
1959	310	75	1,066	9
1960	1,102	5	518	0
1961	563	534	224	17
1962	830	324	207	79
1963	160	765	101	294
Total	9,366	3,548	2,286	399

Index*

Agency for International Development (AID), 49, 55, 75, 118

Agricultural Credit Insurance Fund, 49*n*, 76*n*

Agricultural loans, 55

Agriculture Department: loan agencies in, 4

AID. *See* Agency for International Development

Anti-inflationary monetary policy, 106

Antirecession measures, 72, 94

Area Redevelopment Administration, 2, 123, 124

Area redevelopment loans, 83, 90, 123-24

Bach, G. L., 84*n*

Blitz, Rudolph C., 122*n*

Bloch, Ernest, 2*n*

Bondholders: impact of debt sales on, 34

Borrowers of federal loans: benefits obtained by, 29; increased consumption of, 31; marginal and submarginal groups, 17-18, 38-39, 48, 60, 82, 84; repayments made by, 11, 16

Borrowers in private financial markets, 16, 18, 20, 99

Borrowing. *See* Federal borrowing from private investors

Break, George F., 4*n*, 39*n*, 44*n*, 100*n*

Brill, Daniel H., 41*n*

Bronfenbrenner, Martin, 31*n*

Budget: deficits and surpluses, 10, 11, 22, 23, 24, 25, 44, 59, 60, 61, 64, 65, 66, 67, 68, 70, 73, 97, 105; recommendation for establishment of Federal Lending

* References to tables and charts are in italics.

Account, 5-6; treatment of federal loans in, 4, 5, 10, 39-41

Business cycles: effect of on FHA loans, 93-94; and foreign-aid loans, 118; importance of recognizing turning points in, 125; loans and their fiscal offsets in, 55-81; peaks, troughs, and transitions in, *57;* role of federal lending in, 64; and small business loans, 89-91. *See also* Federal lending in different business cycles

Business loans: reactions to recessions, 89-91; reactions to tight money (1955-57), 86-89

Cabinet Committee on Federal Credit Programs, 27, 28*n*, 41

Canada: Eximbank loans to, 117

College housing loans, 3, 48, 49, 55, 67, 70, 112-14; program stages and time lags in, *112*

Commerce Department, 123, 124*n*

Commission on Money and Credit, 2*n*, 15*n*, 33*n*, 36*n*, 39*n*, 84*n*, 100*n*

Committee for Economic Development, 56*n*

Commodity Credit Corporation, 72*n*

Commodity loans, 117

Community Facilities Administration, 112*n*

Congress: attitudes of toward federal lending, 7, 12; directives of on liquidating the RFC, 91; economy drive of, 60; on increase of taxes, 63-64; loan-granting authority of, 21-22, 51, 94, 114; policies of on mortgages, 106; on reduction of taxes, 58, 65, 73; VA legislation by, 96-97

Construction industry: building activi-

179

ties stimulated by loan programs, 1; business cycle interactions in, 103; FNMA's activities in, 104, 106; prices in, 108. *See also* Home building; Industrial construction

Consumers in the economy: price and income changes as influences on, 30-32

Corporate taxes, 75

Craigie, Stanton, 121*n*

Credit terms, 7, 9, 14, 17, 20, 27, 28, 36, 82, 83, 87, 125

Culbertson, John M., 21*n*, 44*n*, 125*n*

Debt sales of government: to private investors, 20, 28, 29, 34, 43, 81, 82; as source of funds for federal loan programs, 25-26

Defense Department, 47

Defense production loans, 119

Deflationary influences and effects, 16, 21, 25, 31, 100, 110

Denison, Edward F., 56, 56*n*

Development and mutual security loans, 49

Development project loans, 116, 117-18, *119*

Diamond, Arnold H., 45*n*, 113*n*

Direct loan portfolio: percentage increase of (1946-63), 3

Direct loan programs: foreign and defense lending, 47-48, *50;* vs. guaranteed private loans, 72; major groups of, 47-49, *50*, 58; marginal-borrower programs, 48, *50;* subsidiary programs, 48-49, *50;* unrestricted loans, 48, *50*. *See also* Loan programs

Direct loans: debt outstanding by major types of, *4;* and debt trends, 3-4; and economic stabilization, 7-10; in the federal budget, 4-6; vs. federally insured private loans, 67; and resource reallocation, 6. *See also* Direct loan programs

Disaster loans, 3, 49*n*, 83, 87

Disbursements. *See* Loan disbursements

Disposable income, 20, 35, 42

Economy. *See* National economy

Education: President Johnson's Special Message on Poverty, 123; President Kennedy's Message on Education, 122. *See also* National defense educational loans

EIB. *See* Export-Import Bank of Washington

Eisenhower, President Dwight D., 64, 94-95, 114

Electric loan projects. *See* Rural electric and telephone loans

Emergency foreign trade loans, 117

Excise taxes, 60, 65, 72, 75

Eximbank. *See* Export-Import Bank of Washington

Expansionary influences and effects, 17, 18, 21, 22, 27, 28, 35, 79, 100, 110, 111, 126

Expenditures. *See* Federal expenditures

Export-Import Bank of Washington (Eximbank or EIB), 2, 47, 49, 55, 58, 62, 68, 73, 75, 78, 114-16, 116-18, 127*n;* development project and exporter loans, *119;* disbursements by major type of loan, *118*

Exporter loans: long time lag in, 116, 117-18, *119;* stimulated by loan programs, 1. *See also* Export-Import Bank of Washington

Farm Credit Administration, 2

Farm housing loans, 66, 94

Farmers Home Administration (FHA), 2, 4, 48, 49, 55, 66, 68, 77*n*, 92-94, 126*n;* behavior of loans outstanding, *93*

Federal-Aid Highway Act of 1961, 75

Federal borrowing from private investors: as method of financing loan disbursements, 19-20

Federal expenditures: changes in as related to economic indicators, 25; expansion of, 35-36; expansionary powers of purchases of goods and services, 42; major categories of, 41-42; reduction of as method of financing loan disbursements, 19-21, 34

Federal Home Loan Banks, 2, 60

Federal Housing Administration (FHA), 3, 48, 94, 98

Federal lending. *See* all entries under Loan

Federal lending in different business cycles: in expansion periods, 58-60, *59*, 62-64, *63*, 68-70, *69*, 73-75, *74;* monetary importance of, 55-81; in recession and recovery periods, 60-62, *61*, 64-68, *65*, 70-73, *71*, 75-78, *76*

Federal loans outstanding: changes in amount of (1947-62), *79;* during investment boom of 1955-57, 68; rise of in recession of 1958, 70; rise of in recession of 1961-62, 75

Federal National Mortgage Association (FNMA): behavior of in recession and recovery, 105; changes in amounts of loans outstanding (1946-63), *104;* Charter Act of 1954, 97-98; debt-issuing powers of, 2; housing industry served by, 99; loan program of, 49, 62, 82; Management and Liquidation Functions Fund of, 3, 98; maturity of debentures issued by and outstanding (1956-63), *109;* mortgage operations by, 68, 70, 73, 78, 99, 100, 104, 107-11; mortgage purchase commitments of (1948-49), 103; portfolio of, 98*n*, 111; Special Assistance Functions Fund of, 9*n*, 94-95, 96, 98, 126*n;* special functions of, 3, 9*n*. *See also* Secondary Market Operations Trust Fund

Federal Reserve policies and actions, 8, 12, 17, 19, 27, 28*n*, 86, 90

Fellowships and scholarships, compared to student loans, 121

Fels, Rendigs, 28*n*, 96*n*, 113*n*

FHA. *See* Farmers Home Administration; Federal Housing Administration

Financing loan programs: debt-financed loans, 33-34; from general revenues, 2, 25, 26, 82; methods of, 19-22, 30-31, 34, 80

Fiscal offsets generated by federal loans: in appraisal of loan policies, 2; federal use of, 21-27; in FNMA operations, 104; list of, 80; in particular business cycles, 55-81; in purchase of low- and moderate-priced mortgages, 96; wide range of, 19-21

Fiscal policies. *See* Monetary-fiscal policies

FNMA. *See* Federal National Mortgage Association

Foreign aid: commodity loans, 117; development project loans, 116, 117-18, *119;* emergency foreign trade loans, 117; exporter loans, 116-17, 117-18, *119*. *See also* Export-Import Bank of Washington

Foreign and defense lending, 47-48

Full-employment economy, 2, 29, 30, 82, 100-01

Gasoline taxes, 73-74

GNP. *See* Gross National Product

Government loans: advantages of over gifts and grants, 38; allocative effects of on prices and incomes, 29; coordinated with taxing, 31-33; economic impact of compared with federal expenditures and taxes, 41-42; expansionary powers of, 42; incidence of, 28-36; income-output effects of, 14-18, 28; inter- and intraprogram incidence of, 34-36; postwar growth of, 1; vs. public handouts, 38; to small business, 83-86; use of to refinance private loans, 15-16. *See also* Direct loans; and all entries under Loan

Grants and gifts vs. loans, 11, 38, 66

Grebler, Leo, 100*n*, 105, 106*n*

Gross National Product (GNP), 15, 16, 20, 56, 57, 58, 59, 73, 103*n*, 108*n*

Gurley, John G., 59*n*

Guttentag, Jack M., 100*n*, 103*n*

Hall, Robert C., 121*n*

Hansen, W. Lee, 123*n*

Harberger, Arnold C., 30*n*, 100*n*

Health, Education, and Welfare Department, 121*n*, 122*n*

HHFA. *See* Housing and Home Finance Agency

Holmans, A. E., 58*n*, 63*n*, 67*n*

Holzman, F. D., 31*n*

Home building: affected by debt-financed government loans, 33; housing booms in, 62, 102-03, 104; low- and moderate-priced housing mortgages, 94-96; low-rate loans for borrowers entitled to public support, 38; mortgage burden of low-income families, 39; private securities used in, 20; reaction of to monetary ease, 108, 111; reaction of to tight money markets, 106-08; sensitivity of to credit market conditions, 100, 104

House Appropriations Committee, 118n, 123n

House Banking and Currency Committee, 9, 45n

Housing Act of 1961, 96n, 110

Housing and Home Finance Agency (HHFA), 48, 49, 106n, 110n, 112-14, 124n

Housing loans for the elderly, 3, 118

Housing mortgages. See Home building

Huizenga, C. J., 84n

ICA. See International Cooperation Administration

Income. See Disposable income

Income-output effects of loans: activation of money supply, 16; deflationary and expansionary results, 17; impact of on government and private sector, 14; management of through monetary or fiscal policies, 28; private lenders' role in, 15; uses of loan disbursements, 18

Industrial construction, 102-03

Inflationary influences and effects, 31, 84, 101, 125. See also Anti-inflationary monetary policy

Interest rates on loans, 11, 38-39, 66, 87, 89, 90, 93, 111, 112, 116, 125

Internal Revenue Code of 1954, 68

International Cooperation Administration (ICA), 62

Johnson, D. Gale, 2n

Johnson, President Lyndon B., 78, 123

Joint Economic Committee, 59n

Kareken, John, 28n

Kennedy, President John F., 75, 78, 110n, 122

Korean War period, 62, 65, 81, 103; post-Korean period, 117

Labor Department, 122n

Labor surplus areas, 90, 124

Lee, Tong Hun, 21n, 100n

de Leeuw, Frank, 21n

Lending program stages, 51-55; gross loans of five mature programs, 54, 55; net loans of five mature programs, 53, 55; net loans of five youthful programs, 52, 55. See also Loan programs

Lewis, Wilfred, Jr., 23n, 57n, 60n, 66n, 67n, 70n, 72, 95n, 96n

Loan disbursements: as affecting loan repayments, 51; credit flow from, 126; income-output effects of, 16, 18, 23, 24; ratio of to loans outstanding, 54-55; transfer of money involved in, 11

Loan funds: trends in gross and net flows of, 51-55; uses of, 18

Loan principal repayments: borrower's action on, 42; deflationary impact of on the private sector, 16, 17; recommendations for flexibility of, 9; return flow from, 7, 11, 126; stages of in loan program, 51

Loan programs: benefits and burdens imposed by, 29-30, 32, 33, 35; cyclical behavior of, 78-79; defined, 1; direct loan programs, 58 ff.; expansionary powers of, 8; fiscal offsets of federal lending, 19-27; goals of, 36-39; impact of on economy, 1; impact of on federal debts, expenditures, and taxes, 2; individual loan programs, 58 ff.; liquidation of, 58; methods of financing disbursements in, 19; as moderator of economic fluctuations, 83; principal stages of, 51; as profit-making enterprise, 36-37. See also Direct loan programs; Government loans; Lending program stages

Loan sales: by agency and program, 77, 78; to private investors, 2, 10, 40, 66

Loans. See Government loans

McCroskey, John, 84n

McKie, James W., 36n

Maisel, Sherman J., 100n

Marginal- and submarginal-borrower loans. *See* Borrowers of federal loans

Mayer, Thomas, 113*n*

Meltzer, Allan H., 20*n*

Monetary-fiscal policies and effects, 11-14, 21, 22*n*, 27-28, 39-46, 58, 60, 68, 70-71, 73, 82, 84, 86, 92, 105, 106, 108, 110, 125, 126

Money creation as method of financing loan disbursements, 19, 21, 26, 29, 30-31, 43

Money flows produced by loans: on capital and income account, 12-13; in default and liquidation operations, 13-14; effect of on small businesses, 86; in the FHA postwar record, 92-94; in portfolio operations, 13; in the private sector, 80, 86; reverse flows from private sector to government, 64; stages of in ratio of loans outstanding and disbursements, 55; as stimulus to the economy, 16, 58, 78

Money supply in private hands, 36

Moor, Roy E., 24*n*

Mortgages. *See* Federal National Mortgage Association; Home building

Mushkin, Selma J., 122*n*

Muth, Richard F., 100*n*

National Bureau of Economic Research, 56, 105*n*

National Defense Education Act of 1958, 120

National defense educational loans, 2, 48, 55, 83, 120-23, 127

National economy: changing conditions in, 125; contributions of loan programs to stability of, 1; effect of foreign-aid loans on, 118; effect of long-lag loan approval on, 111, 113, 115, 116; growth potential of, 120; impact of federal loan disbursements on, 8, 17-18, 29, 84, 127; and needs of government borrowers, 83; significance of student loan program for, 121; stability of, 82, 94, 119

National security: in consideration of loan applications, 3, 47-48; defense production loans for, 119

Output-generating powers of loans, 14-16. *See also* Income-output effects of loans

Policy makers in loan programs, 2, 8, 10, 12, 26, 42, 67, 102

Postal rate increases, 73

Private financial markets, 15, 16, 28, 35-37, 39, 55, 84-86, 87, 98, 99, 100, 101, 105, 106-11, 116, 124, 125, 127

Private lenders. *See* Private financial markets

Private spending behavior, 19, 20, 32-33

Public Housing Administration, 48, 98*n*

Public works: advances for, 3; economic effects of planning for, 127; loans for constructing public facilities, 3, 124; programs for state and local agencies, 65; redevelopment loans for, 123-24

REA. *See* Rural Electrification Administration

Recession and recovery movements, 27, 44, 64, 65, 79, 84, 92, 115, 116, 125; business loan reactions to, 89-91

Reconstruction Finance Corporation (RFC), 3, 55, 60, 78, 94; liquidation of, 91-92

Repayments. *See* Loan principal repayments

Residential construction. *See* Home building

Resources: impact of loan program on allocation of, 3, 35, 38, 39

Revenue Act of 1948, 58; of 1950, 62

RFC. *See* Reconstruction Finance Corporation

Rolph, Earl R., 30*n*, 34*n*

Rural electric and telephone loans, 2, 66, 114-16; percentages of funds advanced for (1956-60), *115*

Rural Electrification Administration (REA), 4, 5*n*, 48, 49, 55, 62, 66, 70, 112, 114-16; time required for processing loans of, *114*

Samuelson, Paul A., 75

SBA. *See* Small Business Administration

Schlesinger, James R., 15*n*

Schultz, Theodore W., 122n
Secondary Market Operations Trust Fund: compared with direct loan program, 101-02; countercyclical potentialities of, 82, 126; dependence of on private investors, 98; establishment of, 106; expansionary influence of on the economy, 100; limitations of in economic stabilization, 101; money flows of to private sector, 107; mortgage sales by, 96; segregated in the Budget, 72n; stabilization problems of, 99; Treasury investment in, 98. See also Federal National Mortgage Association
Secondary mortgage market operations, 97-111; countercyclical potentialities of, 126; with private funds, 106-11; relation of to business cycles, 102; stabilization problems in, 99-103; with Treasury funds, 98, 103-05. See also Federal National Mortgage Association; Secondary Market Operations Trust Fund
Small Business Act (1958), 89
Small Business Administration (SBA), 85n, 86n, 87n, 124n; and Congress, 66; financial assistance programs of, 48, 49, 83-92; loan approvals and disbursements by, 88; total portfolio of, 83n
Small business development company loans, 3, 83n
Small Business Investment Act (1958), 89
Small business investment company program, 3, 49n, 83, 89n, 127
Small business loans, 3, 83-86, 126n; reactions to recessions, 89-91; reactions to tight money, 86-89
Social benefits of loan programs, 6, 37-38
Social Security: Amendments of 1961, 76n; payroll taxes, 74, 76
Solow, Robert M., 28n
Spending behavior. See Private spending behavior
Stabilizers in the economy, 33, 44, 60, 64, 91, 94, 126; flexible aspects of, 83-97
State and local development company programs, 83
State and local government projects. See Public works

Stockfisch, J. A., 28n
Student Loan Funds, 120-23

Taxation: coordinated and uncoordinated, 31-33
Taxes: determination of, 23, 24; effect of on economic activity, 8, 32; increase of as method of financing loan disbursements, 19-20, 25, 29; reduction of, 22, 25
Taylor, Stephen, 41n
Telephone loan projects. See Rural electric and telephone loans
Temporary Extended Unemployment Compensation Act of 1961, 76n
Time lags between authorization and disbursement of loans, 83, 84, 91, 92, 97, 99; long-lag programs, 8, 9, 111-20, 125
Transfer payments: effect of reduction of, 35; as stimulators of economic activity, 1, 8, 19, 42
Treasury: bond sales of, 19; borrowing rate of, 39; inclusion of interest costs of in lending agency expenses, 6, 45-46; interest rates of, 102; money expenditures by, 13-14; nonaccess to funds of in programs issuing their own securities, 22; on tax reforms, 70n; Treasury-financed FNMA and VA funds, 97-98
Treasury Department, 47
Treasury securities: interest on added to lending agency expenses, 27; maturities of, 26; sales of to private investors, 25
Truman, President Harry S., 58
Turvey, Ralph, 20n

Underemployment and unemployment: effect of loan policies on, 2, 7, 10, 22, 23, 42-44, 65, 66, 76, 78, 83, 89, 94, 95, 102, 103, 108, 110, 111, 120-24, 125. See also Full-employment economy
United Kingdom loan, 49, 58
Unrestricted loans, 48, 59, 60
Urban Renewal Administration, 48
Urban renewal program, 66

VA. See Veterans Administration

Vendee loans, 48n

Veterans Administration (VA), 49, 66, 70, 73, 78, 98, 103n; direct home loans for veterans, 3, 48, 96-97, 126n; guaranteed loans, 3, 96, 97; loan sales campaign of, 97

Vickrey, William, 123n

Welfare aspects of federal lending, 36-39, 46

Wendel, Helmut F., 41n

World War I: loan programs prior to, 1

World War II: debt trends in postwar period, 3-4, 51-55; direct loan program in postwar period, 47-50